Praise for *The Prayer Book for Tired Parents*

The Prayer Book for Tired Parents is an excellent resource for the everyday mother or father who needs encouragement and support in difficult moments. If you just had a baby or have several children, it's refreshing to know you are not alone.

—Crystalina Evert
Author and speaker

This outstanding book is a treasure for tired parents who love the Lord and who, in spite of being tired, want to share that love with their children. It is full of practical ideas and resources to help parents follow the exhortation of the Church in *On Christian Marriage* to "raise up fellow-citizens of the saints and members of God's household."

Debbie and David Cowden see clearly that our children are talents committed to our charge by God to be restored to Him. Now, one cannot choose for one's children, but one can build a foundation of prayer that will help them choose, and that is what this book is designed to do. It explains the value and importance of fundamental Catholic practices, such as enthronement of the Most Sacred Heart of Jesus, consecration to the Blessed Mother and St. Joseph, filling one's home with holy reminders, and building a culture that includes dedicated prayer time, daily Mass, a family litany of saints, and prayer interwoven throughout the day. It gives reasonable suggestions for how to start or enrich those practices.

My experience is that to give what is needed to one's children, one must embrace it oneself. I found the ideas, worksheets, explanations, prayers, and resources in *The Prayer Book for Tired Parents* to be remarkably helpful, insightful, and moving. I think every parent, tired or not, will profit from this book.

—Laura Berquist
Founder of Mother of Divine Grace School

A wealth of Catholic prayers and practices! Journey with Debbie and David as they share many rich devotions and prayer practices and, even better, show how to implement them into your life. As a mother of young children, I was inspired by their dedication and love for the Catholic Faith!

—Emily Jaminet
Author of *Secrets of the Sacred Heart* and
director of Sacred Heart Enthronement Network/
www.WelcomeHisHeart.com

A do-it-yourself prayer kit for all parents striving to grow their family in holiness while bleary-eyed and oh, so tired. An honest account of the realities of family life, Debbie and Dave's *Prayer Book for Tired Parents* will undoubtedly be the go-to resource for generations of parents. Every home needs a copy within reach and at least one copy to give to family and friends.

—Paola Ciskanik
Founder of Catholic Homeschool Community

As someone who knows what it's like to be tired, I recognize the wisdom of the Cowdens' words. This is a rich treasury of Catholic devotions, practices, and tips on how to parent in a healthy, holy way. All things are possible with the grace of God, but often, God waits to be asked before He gives us the grace. The Cowdens show you how to live in relationship with God, the Church, and your family all at the same time, come riches or poverty, come mess or tidiness, come tiredness or rest. This book will be a great aid to those who are looking for answers!

—Very Rev. Chris Alar, M.I.C.
Director of the Association of Marian Helpers
and Provincial Superior, Marian Fathers,
United States and Argentina

Readable, funny, poignant, and full of practical wisdom. As tired parents ourselves, we greatly appreciate this resource by David and Debbie Cowden!

—Jackie and Bobby Angel
Authors and speakers

This book is an indispensable resource for the tired and overwhelmed parent. David and Debbie Cowden have created a beautiful guide that will help you find your way back to peace and sanity.

—Jen Fulwiler
Stand-up comic and best-selling author of *Something Other Than God*

I've known Debbie since her early days at EWTN, nearly a decade ago and have watched her strive to practice Mother Angelica's spirituality as a wife and mother. In *The Prayer Book for Tired Parents*, she and David apply the wisdom of the saints to the highs and lows of parenthood—helping all to follow Mother Angelica's famous exhortation: "We are all called to be great saints. Don't miss the opportunity." I'm sure Reverend Mother would be proud.

—Raymond Arroyo
New York Times best-selling author of *Mother Angelica*; creator and host of EWTN's *The World Over*; and *Fox News* analyst

The Prayer Book for Tired Parents is a gentle guide for parents with young children, encouraging parents to develop a *real* spiritual life for the family in a way that doesn't feel like a burden and won't lead to burnout. Dave and Debbie's tips make it feel possible for busy families to be holy families.

—Chris Stefanick
Founder and president of Real Life Catholic

This book is honest and down-to-earth. If you are a parent, or a parent-to-be, and you have the desire to keep God first in your life and in the lives of your spouse and children, you need to keep this book close at hand. It is filled with practical tips on how to make prayer a priority and on how to pray, and it includes all sorts of prayers that you can weave into the daily fabric of your family life. It also gives the tired parent a lot of understanding, encouragement, and motivation to get up and just keep going. Excellent job, Dave and Debbie!

—John S. Martignoni
Founder and president of the Bible Christian Society
and author of *Blue Collar Apologetics*

To paraphrase G. K. Chesterton, a sharp-eyed social observer: if prayer is worth doing, it is worth doing tired. Making more time for God as you make more time for your children is more doable than exhausted parents know. *The Prayer Book for Tired Parents* is chock-full of ways and times to touch the face of God as you touch the face of your children.

—Dr. Ray Guarendi
Catholic psychologist, author, and speaker

The Prayer Book for Tired Parents

DAVID AND DEBBIE COWDEN

The Prayer Book for Tired Parents

Practical Ways to Grow in Love of God and Get Your Family to Heaven

EWTN Publishing, Inc.
Irondale, Alabama

Printed in the United States of America

Cover design by Valerie Delgado with Sophia Institute Press.

Cover art: *The Holy Family* © 2022 Valerie Delgado.

EWTN Publishing, Inc.
5817 Old Leeds Road, Irondale, AL 35210

Distributed by Sophia Institute Press, Box 5284, Manchester, NH 03108.

paperback ISBN 978-1-68278-287-3

ebook ISBN 978-1-68278-288-0

Library of Congress Control Number: 2022944590

First printing

For our children,

the reason we are tired parents,

and

in thanksgiving for the spiritual motherhood of

Mother Mary Angelica, PCPA

By reason of their dignity and mission, Christian parents have the specific responsibility of educating their children in prayer, introducing them to gradual discovery of the mystery of God and to personal dialogue with Him:

> It is particularly in the Christian family, enriched by the grace and the office of the sacrament of Matrimony, that from the earliest years children should be taught, according to the faith received in Baptism, to have a knowledge of God, to worship Him and to love their neighbor.

The concrete example and living witness of parents is fundamental and irreplaceable in educating their children to pray.

Only by praying together with their children can a father and mother—exercising their royal priesthood—penetrate the innermost depths of their children's hearts and leave an impression that the future events in their lives will not be able to efface.

—Pope St. John Paul II, *Familiaris Consortio*, no. 60

Contents

PART 3

Stepping Forward in Faith

PART 4

Prayers and Reflections on the Saints

Foreword

You must have picked up this book because you are tired. God willing, you are not tired of your spouse and your children! You are just plain tired. You probably never realized that marriage and family life could drain you. You might have thought your spouse would be your completion and would fulfill the deepest desires of your heart. You might have had an ideal family in mind, and things might not be the way you planned.

As a good friend of mine says, "your spouse is the diagnosing finger that God wills to heal your infirmities." Through the sacrament of Marriage, and through bearing its fruits, children, the Lord wills to heal you. When we have physical pain and the doctor presses in on the spot, it hurts! There might be issues in your life that have arisen within the context of marriage and parenting that you never knew about. And you are tired!

Again, you might not be tired of your marriage and your family but might be tired of *being tired*. It's okay to admit you are tired. You don't have to feel stuck. Sometimes we feel caught in quicksand and don't know how to get out. Many people go for long bouts of time without even telling their spouses how they feel, often out of fear of rejection or judgment: Would my spouse still love me if he or she knew how I felt?

When a man and woman are united in the sacrament of Marriage, the two become one flesh. Your thinking shifts from saying "I" to "we." Maybe you found it easy at first. As life goes on, the pressure turns up. Life circumstances come. Sometimes family conflicts enter into the picture. And it's not always pretty. It can exhaust you.

I have known Dave and Debbie Cowden since they were long-distance dating in 2013. I've never met a couple who put so much effort into their relationship—from the very beginning, desiring that their relationship be dedicated to Christ. They were honest with each other.

I think they would be honest and tell you that marriage and family life have tested them in every way—in a good way! But they daily strive to live out their commitment to Christ, to each other, and to their precious children. And they will tell you: "It's tiring!"—and say it with joy!

This book is their attempt to share some things that they have discovered from the treasury of the Church. Dave and Debbie love each other, and they love being married. I believe that every married couple has something beautiful to offer the Church and even the world. And the beauty is magnified with the creation of each precious child conceived. Every family is unique and part of a tapestry that will form the Face of Christ at the end of time. Even in the messiness. Even in the brokenness.

Within these pages, you will find priceless gems from the lives of the saints and from two very tired parents. After reading Dave and Debbie's book, you may realize that you have stories, prayers, and devotions that are a part of your narrative. Your story is different from the Cowdens' story.

I'm proud of Dave and Debbie and how I've been able to witness the life of Christ lived in their marriage and family life. I pray that in some unique way, this book will bless your marriage and family too.

Fr. John Paul Mary Zeller, MFVA
Franciscan Missionaries of the Eternal Word
Irondale, Alabama

Preface

An important note about this book: Although technically it is written by Debbie and *David Cowden, we've decided to present the material in one voice—Debbie's, for the sake of clarity.*

I wish someone had given us a book like this when our first child was born.

As new parents, we were completely shell-shocked by the drastic change in our lives with the addition of our daughter. I suppose we anticipated getting less sleep. We prepared for the financial aspect of parenting. We thought about how babies fit into our career goals and where we wanted to live.

But we never considered how becoming parents would change our prayer lives.

We didn't consider how we'd pray, how long we'd pray, where we'd pray, whether we'd utilize the parish's cry room, and so on.

No one had told us about this. How could we have known?

As we've made more Catholic parent friends, we've realized this is a common problem. Many Catholic parents are struggling to navigate passing the Faith along to their children—and for a number of reasons: busy family life, poor catechesis, no model for passing on the Faith, and so on.

The weight of the responsibility to raise children in the Faith, as promised at Baptism, is compounded by the already tremendous responsibility of keeping the kids fed, clothed, bathed, and educated. No wonder so many parents are tired!

This book is designed for everyday Catholic parents in the pews—particularly, new parents and parents with young kids.

If you want to grow in your love of God and get your family to Heaven but are impossibly tired and don't even know where to begin, let us help by reintroducing you to the beauty, goodness, and joy of your Catholic Faith.

The Prayer Book for Tired Parents includes traditional prayers and popular devotions for Catholics. It includes the Cowdens' pro tips for building a foundation of prayer and growing in love of God. It includes brief reflections on saints whom parents can befriend and turn to for help. It includes simple go-to prayers for the everyday joys and struggles of parenting. And it includes a wealth of resources for building a foundation of prayer for your family.

We hope this book will help you develop concrete habits of prayer, reignite your love of your Catholic Faith as you practice it in everyday life, and build the spiritual endurance to pursue a deeper relationship with God. And, most importantly, we hope you'll be well on your way to fulfilling the first responsibility of parenting: to get your family to Heaven.

Please be assured of our prayers for you, fellow tired parent. You are not in this alone! May the grace and peace of our good God be with you as you begin this journey, and may He grant you the patience and perseverance to lead your family to Him.

In Christ,
Dave and Debbie Cowden

INTRODUCTION

Get to Know the Cowdens

We are all called to be great saints. Don't miss the opportunity!

—Mother Angelica, Foundress of EWTN Global Catholic Network

In the one short quotation above, Mother Angelica sums up the call to holiness we all share and the reason David (whom we'll now refer to as Dave) and I wrote this book.

We both watched EWTN before we started dating. I was a cradle Catholic, and he was converting to the Faith when we met in college. Though we came from different walks of life, Mother Angelica's mission of EWTN changed both of us.

As part of that mission for nearly a decade, the Cowdens have made appearances on the network, and viewers have seen glimpses of us doing our best to live out Mother's spirituality—to be holy in our state of life, to be docile to God's will, and to find the joy and the humor in God's plan.

Dave and I were dating long-distance when I started working for EWTN in 2013. I served as a TV series and live-show producer for the daily Mass, papal events, *At Home with Jim and Joy*, *Life on the Rock*, *The Catholic View for Women*, *Blue Collar Apologetics*, and others. I field-produced EWTN's live coverage of the March for Life, the Walk for Life West Coast, and the World Meeting of Families in Philadelphia.

After getting married in 2015 and having our first baby in 2016, I became EWTN's social-media coordinator and Dave began his doctoral program. I began co-hosting *EWTN Religious Catalogue* on the same set Mother Angelica used when she hosted the show.

In the summer of 2018, I announced on *EWTN Religious Catalogue* the news of our second baby. Viewers watched me get bigger and bigger as our little boy grew bigger and bigger in my womb.

In 2019, Dave and I moved home to Ohio with our toddler and our newborn. Dave began his career in health care, and I continued as a digital-media specialist for EWTN, managing the network's social media, writing feature articles for the EWTN *Wings* weekly e-mail newsletter, and appearing seasonally on *EWTN Religious Catalogue*.

In 2020, right before the pandemic, while co-hosting EWTN's live coverage of the March for Life, I announced the news of our third baby. And since then, I've remained on the front lines of the battle for souls on social media, helping fellow Catholics grow in their Faith while helping my own family during these difficult times.

It truly has been a blessing for Dave and me to be part of the EWTN family. It has changed our lives and shaped the way we parent. We are immersed in Mother Angelica's mission and have adopted her way of holiness—doing everything for the love of Jesus, recognizing how God uses our weakness for His glory, and striving to be holy where we are.

Mother Angelica told viewers, "I want you to have a new concept of holiness. You've got to be holy where you are: washing the dishes, at the office, at school. Where you are, you can be holy there."

For many of us, this means being holy in the throes of parenthood. But if holy parenthood wasn't modeled in our youth, it might seem impossible or unfathomable to attain now. If we're judging our parenting success by the skewed concept of parenting that we see on social media, we're bound to face discouragement. If we're constantly keeping busy with activities outside our home and not prioritizing our spiritual life, we're bound to face burnout.

As Mother Angelica said, "We are all called to be great saints. Don't miss the opportunity!"

Parenting is hard, no matter how you look at it. You're called to be a holy parent, even if you're a *tired* parent. As you read this book, I hope you gain insight into the good fruit that comes from being a tired parent.

I hope you can see how hard it is to try to be holy and how it isn't shameful to admit that the pursuit can be tiring.

I hope you make use of the devotions and prayers included in these pages and even come up with some of your own.

And I hope you don't miss the opportunity to grow in your love of God and will one day celebrate with your entire family of saints in Heaven.

PART 1

Motivation for Tired Parents

1

A Tired Parent's Call to Holiness

We shall not waste our time in looking for extraordinary experiences in our life of contemplation but live by pure faith, ever watchful and ready for His coming by doing our day-to-day duties with extraordinary love and devotion.[1]

—St. Mother Teresa of Calcutta

When I was in college, I did it all. I was the quintessential eager coed who stacked my schedule with classes, student organizations, and internships. I was a resident adviser (Resident Adviser of the Year, that is); radio co-host; TV producer, anchor, and host; tutor; student sacristan; and nominee for homecoming court; and I was numbered among The "Top 1 Percent of On-Campus Leaders." I maintained a 4.0 GPA for almost my entire college "career" and graduated with honors. I worked numerous part-time jobs throughout college—teaching acting and modeling classes, working as a production assistant for the local public-television

[1] Mother Teresa, *No Greater Love* (Novato, CA: New World Library, 1997), "On Prayer."

station, managing a house-painting franchise, working in the mall, nannying, and freelancing. I interned for two major television networks, including one in Times Square in New York City. I thought I was unstoppable.

After graduation, I immediately accepted a full-time job as a TV producer for EWTN while working several other jobs to repay my student loans so my husband and I could begin our marriage debt-free. I was a hostess at one restaurant, a server at another, and a part-time youth minister, and I also took on freelance video and photography gigs.

I'm now a full-time, work-from-home mom with three young kids and, remarkably, I am more tired *now* than I've been at any other point in my life.

I'm not just tired. There are times when I am 100 percent exhausted. I'm pushed to the limit, stretched thin, depleted, and, occasionally, completely burned out.

Parenting is the hardest thing I've ever done. I don't get evenings or weekends off or summer vacations. I don't get *any* holidays off. One Mother's Day, I was in a cherry picker, painting our centennial home's dormers while in my second trimester. But that's another story for another day.

Maybe it's the perpetual sleepless nights. Maybe it's the bouts of screaming peppered throughout the day that quickly wear on me. Maybe it's the fact that I've not yet been able to get all three kids to nap at the same time so I can enjoy a nap. (Oh, how I miss naps!) Maybe it's the fact that I've been pregnant or nursing, or both, almost the entire time I've been married.

Yes, I'm more tired now than I've been at any point in my life, but I'm also more fulfilled now than I've been at any point in my life. I'm a tired parent, and I'm not afraid to admit it. And here's why:

- I'm tired because God blessed Dave and me with three babies in five years, and I'm grateful to have them.
- I'm tired because I hardly get a minute to myself, but that's because my arms have been filled with children who want to nurse and cuddle.
- I'm tired because my children are energetic and want me to play with them.
- I'm tired because my kindergarten daughter wants to stay up late crafting with me, and we get so caught up making artwork and memories that we stay up hours past her bedtime.
- I'm tired because my work-life balance sometimes gets skewed, but we are providing for our family. We have everything we need and plenty that we want.
- I'm tired because the laundry and dishes never end, but we have clean, hot, running water.
- I'm tired because I'm doing everything in my power to shield my kids from the ugliness of sin, to raise them in the Faith, and to prepare them to change the world with the help of God's grace.

I'm a *tired parent*. It might sound like self-deprecation, but my husband and I have learned to embrace this description for several reasons.

First, it takes the pressure off us. We don't have to spend energy pretending we are not exhausted beyond belief. After all, anyone who has raised kids will tell you it is not for the faint of heart.

Second, it gives us a glimpse of the Father's love for us. Moments in parenting allow us to understand better our own spiritual infancy and the patience God shows us every day. Sure, God's not tired, but I bet we test His patience regularly! God loves us not for what we do for Him or what we're capable of but because we are His children. Though we are physically and mentally tired, we can find rest and peace when we fall into His arms.

Third, it changes the way we pray. Instead of asking God for certain favors, we are learning abandonment, trust, hope, charity, selflessness, and humility. What we pray for and how we pray are completely different from how we prayed before having children.

Finally, being tired reminds us parents that we are doing important work. It is exhausting, it is difficult, it is an incredible responsibility—and God bestowed it upon *you*. (No pressure!) Everything we do is for God.

If you're a tired parent, that's OK. If you can embrace this description, you're going to be changed forever. The goal of this book is to help you use your vocation and state of life for God's glory, no matter how tired you are. But it doesn't come easily, or naturally, given the stressors and distractions that plague tired parents.

We wrote this book primarily for parents with children under the age of ten, but the principles apply to parents at any stage. It's never too late to help your family grow in holiness! This book is for the average family in the pew, trying to be holy and trying to live the Faith.

- It's for parents who are trying. Those who bring their children to Mass on Sundays, even though they have a hard time paying attention.
- It's for families who aren't yet praying the Rosary daily.
- It's for families who have rarely or never attended daily Mass.

- It's for the parents who were raised Catholic but never had a solid example of what it looks like to live the Faith.
- It's for parents who have just baptized their child and are unsure of what to do next.
- It's also for parents who are converts and are trying to dive deep into the Catholic Faith. (Welcome, by the way! We're happy to have you!)
- It's for the parents who are reverts or reverts-in-the-making, who lived outside the Faith for years and have returned. (Welcome back! We're happy to have you!)

This book is not for those who know everything about the Faith and not for those who are already living the Faith perfectly. If that is you, congratulations!

This is not a parenting book. It's a book on prayer. We're not going to tell you how to raise your kids, what to feed them, how to discipline them, or how to educate them.

We aim to show you how to make prayer a priority in your life. We will introduce you to a new mindset when it comes to embracing your vocation and offering every moment of your day to God. We will show you how, through prayer, the sacraments, and holy reminders, you can change your life as you pursue closeness with God. You are made for communion with God, even if you don't know what that means right now.

It's not going to make your life easier, but perhaps it will make it more fruitful. It's not going to take away the stuff that makes you want to tear your hair out—picky eaters, endless laundry and dishes, sleepless nights, sibling squabbles, and so on—but perhaps these things will no longer drain you as they do now.

It's not going to take away the suffering you experience—from miscarriage, child loss, infertility, financial strain, family strain, marital strain—but perhaps it will show you how to place your crosses at the foot of Our Lord's Cross and remind you that you're not alone.

I won't lie; I have plenty of days on which I watch the clock, waiting to pass off the kids to my husband. Some days, he comes home to a frazzled wife and no prospects for dinner.

We're recovering from a major traumatic event that forced us from our home and caused extraordinary loss.

We've been through bitter challenges in our marriage that have tested our faith and torn open old wounds.

We're battling health concerns for multiple family members, with no clear answers in sight.

We're experiencing regular bouts of isolation due to limited family support and the absence of the "village" that families used to rely on "back in the day."

We're living through a global pandemic and global unrest. And that's in addition to the everyday struggles of raising children in an increasingly secular culture, which hates the nuclear family.

These are all things that drain parents, and some days, we feel completely helpless. Maybe you've been there too. Every family has a unique set of difficult circumstances, but there are many similarities in the overarching struggles.

When Dave and I started sharing about our difficulties with other Catholic parents, we realized they struggled too. It turns out that many couples—especially parents with young children—lack balance between work and family life. They don't know how to orient their days around prayer. They endure family issues and struggle to love God through living their vocation to the fullest.

Our friends shared our desire for holiness, not knowing where to begin or how to be consistent.

And even while practicing the habits of prayer we mention in this book, it's still hard and we're still tired.

The difference is that we know that we're bearing good fruit for our souls and those of our children because we're trying to love God more. We're abandoning ourselves more to God, and it has made things better for us. Instead of being helplessly tired and discouraged, as we had been in the past, we can now see how our everyday pursuit of holiness fits into God's big picture for our lives. We are finding more joy in practicing our Faith, knowing we're doing the right things to help our family become saints.

But what are the "right things" to help our kids grow in holiness, and how can we do them when we're tired? Where do we even begin?

Let's be practical

Where are you now in your spiritual life, and where would you like to be?

Pro tip

Be honest and specific. Put this in writing to reference later.

Why am I reading this book?

Are God and prayer the highest priority in our life? If not, who or what is?

What would it look like if our family truly lived our Faith to the fullest?

"Saints are ordinary people, who do what they do for the love of Jesus, say what they must say without fear, love their neighbor when they are cursed by him, and live without regret over yesterday or fear of tomorrow." (Mother Angelica)

2

The Purpose and Format of This Book

You either belong wholly to the world or wholly to God.[2]

—St. John Vianney

When Dave proposed to me, he gave me two gifts. The first, of course, was the ring. The second was a home study kit to help me repay tens of thousands of dollars of student debt I accrued while trying to "do it all." I know—he's *super* romantic.

The kit contained a set of DVD courses with a companion workbook, a memoir from the financial guru who compiled the course, various worksheets, and a progress chart. The course was designed to help people like me repay debt, build savings, and ultimately attain financial security. I thought I knew enough about money already, but I didn't yet possess the self-control to manage

[2] St. Jean-Marie Vianney, *Sermons of the Cure of Ars: Sermons for All the Sundays and Feast Days of the Year* (Charlotte, NC: TAN Books, 2013), Twenty-Third Sunday after Pentecost: "No Man Can Serve Two Masters."

my money well, nor did I have a grasp on the big financial picture. I couldn't be successful with money because I didn't even know where to begin.

We wasted no time in getting started. Dave and I watched the videos together and decided we were going to change our lives forever—together. We created budgets (separate budgets because we were not married yet and he lived six hundred miles away), discussed goals, held each other accountable, and noted every transaction during our regular check-ins. We cut our spending and accounted for every penny, and I threw every spare dollar at my student loans. I picked up extra shifts at my part-time jobs, knowing that every dollar had a purpose. Suddenly, it all felt worth it. And every month, I'd submit extra payments to my online loan repayment service. The loan balance continued to fall. And we did it! My last loan was repaid three months before our wedding, and we started our marriage debt-free!

I'm saying this not to brag but to make an important point. You can't meet goals if you do not have objective steps to attain them. The program we used has specific steps for each part of the financial journey. They offer clear dos and don'ts for healthy money habits. The rules are strict, but they make sense, and they work! And they help transform your life so financial wellness becomes second nature. Our kids likely will never experience their mom's embarrassing financial faux pas. They'll have healthy models of money management from the beginning. We've changed our family's future by working on these habits for more than seven years.

The same principles apply to our spiritual lives. There are specific steps we take to build good prayer habits, avoid sinful habits, develop virtue, and reorient our lives toward Heaven. We're going to show you where and how to start, and you'll be able to use this book to make a concrete plan for cultivating a strong prayer life for your family.

But that's not to say that simply doing what we tell you to do is going to make you a saint. No, not at all. The primary reason you are doing this is to grow in your love of God: to know Him more, to love Him more, and to serve Him more. How can we say we love God if we never spend time with Him in prayer? How can we say we love God if we don't give ourselves entirely to Him?

What we share in this book will help open your heart to God's graces in ways you might never have known possible and will show you how to develop and deepen your relationship with God. These are the tried-and-true devotions and practices that have made countless saints over the past two thousand years.

This book is meant to be used daily as a means of guidance and fortification. It is like a springboard for infusing prayer into every part of your day, so your family can truly become saints. We offer guidance on building habits of prayer as well as adjusting routines to make more room for God.

Let's be practical

Do not be afraid to write in this book, dog-ear or tear out pages, or send screenshots to your friends. It is a book that is made to be used, and the more you use it, the more you will find you are absorbing and incorporating it into everyday life.

Pro tip

Commit to reading and rereading this book daily as you build habits of prayer.

Are my spouse and I ready to make the changes necessary to grow in our love of God and get our family to Heaven?

What fears and concerns do we have?

How much time and effort are we willing to commit to our own holiness and that of our family?

"God wants us to do great things for Him, and the greatest thing of all is our own holiness." (Mother Angelica)

3

"The Spirit Is Willing, but the Flesh Is Weak"

If I had to summarize my prayer life in one sentence, it would be this: "The spirit is willing, but the flesh is weak" (see Matt. 26:41). I imagine this is the case for many parents, who feel they are merely "scraping by" or "surviving, and not thriving." Yes, these are clichés. Yes, they ring true.

We Cowdens have seen this in our lives. There are seasons when our family prays regularly together and other seasons when we feel we hardly resemble a Catholic family, outside of attending Sunday Mass.

It was not always like this. It is humbling to compare our lives as parents with our lives before having three children.

When we began dating in college, Dave used to visit my residence hall after classes, and we would pray and read Scripture together. We would make holy hours at the university's Catholic chapel. We read books alongside each other, and I would zero in on the pages he had dog-eared and the sections he had highlighted.

After our wedding, Dave was an altar server at EWTN's daily Mass, and we taught an eighth-grade Confirmation class together. We dreamed about how perfect and holy our future Catholic children would be.

What a wake-up call we've had!

God has given us three wonderful little Catholic children, but they're not "holy" in the way we planned, and that is partly due to our shortcomings as parents. Our eldest, who is five years old at the time of writing this book, insists on squirming in the pew, whispering very loudly during Mass, and complaining when she doesn't like the music. Our three-year-old son can barely make it through the homily before Dave has to haul him out to the narthex. And the jury is still out on our youngest, who is only a toddler but already has discovered the thrill of hearing her babbles echo through an otherwise quiet church—in the middle of Mass, of course.

But they are holy children in their own special ways. If she is not tired, hungry, or in a feud with her little brother, our eldest genuflects reverently when entering and exiting the pew. During the Elevation, she closes her eyes and whispers, "My Lord and my God!" She stole my chapel veil because she wanted to wear one too. She invokes St. Anthony regularly for his intercession in finding her lost toys, and he listens! She cries when we talk about Baby Jesus sleeping in the manger because there was no room for Him in the inn. She hates the idea of sin. She volunteers to do extra chores around the house so she can earn money to "save the babies." After every Mass, she insists on lighting candles and praying before the statues of the Blessed Mother and St. Joseph. And she recently told me she wants to be a doctor, like her namesake, St. Gianna Molla.

In March 2020, when the Covid lockdowns began and churches closed, my early-rising son and I started watching

EWTN's televised daily Mass together. Some of his first words were "Mass," "Rosary," "Amen," and "Father Mark" (which came out as "Fah Mah"). His ears perk up when Fr. Joseph begins the EWTN Family Prayer. He even surprised me one morning by making the Sign of the Cross: "Fah, Suh, Hah-sa, AMEN!" And he enthusiastically follows along while we read children's books on saints together. He has developed a fondness for Pope St. John Paul II, thanks to some children's books and toys we have. He doesn't quite understand who these holy men and women are yet, but he will one day!

And, again, the jury is still out on our third child, but with a name like Frances Clare and with the influence of her siblings, surely there's hope for her, right? She recognizes "Mama Mary" in art around our house and thinks every baby is Jesus. Since every baby is made in the image and likeness of God, I guess she's not wrong!

Despite what we feel are our weaknesses and failings as *tired parents*, our kids somehow have managed to retain some of the Faith. That wouldn't have happened if we never tried.

Yes, "the spirit is willing, but the flesh is weak." That's our human nature. Even Jesus' closest friends could not stay awake with Him for one hour while He prayed (Matt. 26:40), but He didn't give up on them, and He hasn't given up on us.

From our own spiritual journey, we realized that our "flesh" is always going to be weak. There will always be more we could have done to help our kids grow in holiness. There will always be times when we let God down or let our kids down. When "the spirit is willing," however, we invite God into our homes and open our hearts to receive the grace to be good parents—grace that we can receive only from God; the grace that ultimately saves our children's souls.

With a willing spirit, we open the doors to our homes and give the Holy Spirit room to work. In the following chapters, we will look at specific things we can do to awaken and nurture a willing spirit—such as displaying "holy reminders" and dedicating time to prayer. These make it easier for us as tired parents to practice and pass on the Faith.

And with a spirit of humility, we can abandon ourselves to the will of God. We can do nothing without Him, and everything we are comes from Him. Therefore, in our spiritual journey, we should always strive to seek His will and confidently trust in His goodness and mercy.

Let's be practical

Pray the Litany of Humility daily!

Pro tip

Set an alarm on your phone to pray the Litany of Humility daily, or make it part of your routine to pray it first thing in the morning. Pick one or two lines that resonate with you ("From the desire of being praised, deliver me, Jesus"), and continue praying that line throughout the day.

Litany of Humility

V. Jesus, meek and humble of heart,
R. *Hear me.*

V. From the desire of being esteemed,
R. *Deliver me, Jesus.*

V. From the desire of being loved …
R. *Deliver me, Jesus.*
From the desire of being extolled …
From the desire of being honored …
From the desire of being praised …
From the desire of being preferred to others …
From the desire of being consulted …
From the desire of being approved …
From the fear of being humiliated …
From the fear of being despised …
From the fear of suffering rebukes …
From the fear of being calumniated …
From the fear of being forgotten …
From the fear of being ridiculed …
From the fear of being wronged …
From the fear of being suspected …

V. That others may be loved more than I,
R. *Jesus, grant me the grace to desire it.*
That others may be more esteemed than I …
That, in the opinion of the world, others may increase and I may decrease …
That others may be chosen and I set aside …
That others may be praised and I go unnoticed …
That others may be preferred to me in everything …

That others may become holier than I, provided that I may become as holy as I should …

Lord, grant me the grace of humility and charity, that I may love God above all things for Himself and be ready to renounce all created things rather than offend Him by serious sin. Amen.

"Isn't it a beautiful thing to know and realize that God's power works through you in your weakness?" (Mother Angelica)

4

The Saints Were Tired Parents Too

O Jesus, I promise You to submit myself to all that You permit to happen to me, make me only know Your will.[3]

—St. Gianna Beretta Molla

If you want proof that tired parents can become saints, you're in luck, because there are quite a few of them.

We tend to forget that there are a number of saints who were parents during their earthly lives. They are honored as part of the Church Triumphant today, but only after facing tremendous hardships during their earthly lives:

- Mother Mary and St. Joseph traveled to Egypt, immediately after having a baby, to flee an evil king's attempts to kill their newborn, the Divine Child Jesus, the Savior of the World.

[3] Quoted in Pietro Molla, *Saint Gianna Molla: Wife, Mother, Doctor*, trans. James G. Colbert (San Francisco: Ignatius Press, 2004), 136.

- St. Monica prayed for years for the conversion of both her husband and her wayward son Augustine, who had joined a heretical cult, lived promiscuously, and even fathered a child out of wedlock.

- Sts. Louis and Zélie Martin had a house full of little girls. Don't you think they were tired? You don't have to guess because in the letters St. Zélie wrote to her beloved husband, she made sure he knew just how tired she was! "Oh well, that's the day so far, and it's still only Noon. If this continues, I will be dead by this evening! You see, at the moment, life seems so heavy for me to bear, and I don't have the courage because everything looks black to me."[4]

- St. Gianna Molla was a full-time working mom. She was a physician with three children underfoot and a fourth on the way.

- St. Jane Frances de Chantal was the mother of six. Three of her children died in infancy. She took in the three children of her deceased sister. Then her husband died. She faced family drama with her father-in-law. She experienced horrible mental anguish and spiritual dryness, another son's death, the plague, a daughter-in-law's death, a son-in-law's death, and the pains associated with starting a religious order.

- St. Elizabeth Ann Seton and her husband had five children. After Elizabeth's husband died, financial strains forced her

[4] Blessed Zélie and Louis Martin, *A Call to Deeper Love: The Family Correspondence of the Parents of Saint Thérèse of the Child Jesus (1864–1885)* (Staten Island, NY: Alba House, 2011), letter 132.

to take in his younger six siblings, ages seven to seventeen. As a widow, she founded an academy to support herself and her children.

- St. Basil the Elder and St. Emmelia raised ten children. Anyone with ten children likely knows what it means to be tired. Yet they persevered, and five of their children are now venerated as saints.
- St. Thomas More had four children with his first wife, who died six years into their marriage. He then married a widow with one child and eventually took in two more children—all while serving as Lord Chancellor for the king's court. Are we pretending he wasn't tired? Why are we not mentioning how tired he must have been?

And that is only a few of many!

We needn't, and shouldn't, feel guilty about being tired. Parenting is difficult! Think of all the prayers offered up by these saints, particularly related to their parenting woes. Their lives and actions show us that if God calls us to the vocation of parenthood, He surely will give us the graces to raise our children to be saints, if only we ask for those graces. Look at the good He accomplishes through parents who overcome such suffering. God is using us too.

All ye holy men and women of God, pray for us!

Let's be practical

This book contains reflections on saints whom parents can befriend. Take a moment each day to call upon one saint to accompany you throughout the day. See how their intercession helps you seek God in all things!

Pro tip

Hang prayers and images of the saints throughout your house, where you will see them and remember to pray for their help.

"Men are not born saints with special gifts and privileges. They fight against the world, the flesh, and the devil, and as they conquer, the Spirit of Jesus begins to shine through with more clarity." (Mother Angelica)

5

Put God First, No Matter What

Being children of such a Father, how can we have any other thought than loving Him and serving Him? Be attentive to take care of yourself and your family according to His will, and do not worry about anything else. If you do this, you will see that Jesus is taking care of you.[5]

—St. Padre Pio of Pietrelcina

Love God first and put Him first—always. No matter what. God must be at the center of your family, and loving Him must be the reason for everything you do. If not, nothing else will matter, and nothing will fall into place anyway, since all you were made for is to love God. Your life will not make sense and you'll never truly be at peace if your focus isn't on loving Him.

The first step in growing in holiness as a parent is to understand that everything we do ought to be for the love of God. We're not simply going through the motions of being Catholic. That isn't

[5] Letter to Antonietta Vona, November 15, 1917, quoted in *Padre Pio's Spiritual Direction for Every Day* (Cincinnati: Franciscan Media, 2011), 2.

love. That's acting. And though we will never be able to love God perfectly while on earth, we still are called to love Him more and more each day.

In our vocation as spouses and parents, we do this through our sacramental union with our spouse and the nurturing of our children. We pray together and practice the Faith, rooting out vices and habitual sins, growing in virtue, and showing God's love to our family members. It is not easy, but it is worth it.

But what about every other part of parenting and family life? Growing in the love of God and striving for holiness completely changes my perspective on parenting and allows me to see the other responsibilities in their proper places.

For example, instead of being hyperfocused on raising my kids to be compliant and clean at all times for the sake of having an orderly home, I'm seeing my parental role as one who shepherds my children and shows them the way to the Father. Our relationship is built on love, trust, and the foundations of faith, as opposed to punishment, fear, and worldly expectations.

Sure, I want my house to be clean—doesn't every parent? Sure, I want my kids to eat their vegetables. Sure, I want the laundry to be washed, folded, and put away all on the same day. Sure, I want my kids to go to bed easily at the end of the day. Sure, I want the dishes and floors to clean themselves automatically and never be caked with dried food. Sure, I want my kids to get good grades and excel at their hobbies.

But all these things are not the most important part of parenting. The most important thing about parenting is getting my children to Heaven. I want my kids to love God and to know they are loved by God. I want them to be saints. I want them to be people of virtue. I want to be a person of virtue. If that is truly my primary goal, look at how the expectations change:

- I work on keeping my house clean because I'm thankful for this home and because having a tidy home frees me from worldly distractions.
- I understand my toddlers don't want to eat their vegetables because they're in the normal developmental phase when they tend to be defiant as they explore their own bodily autonomy and independence. This is a great time to start introducing them to basic concepts of Theology of the Body, in which they learn to love and wonder at their amazing God-given bodies, which are fueled by the variety of foods God created for us.
- I'm thankful for my washer and my dryer, and all the clothes my family members wear. I'm thankful for the income we have that allows us to buy whatever clothes we need. I'm going to take some extra kids' clothing to the St. Vincent de Paul clothing store so another family can use them.
- Another day has passed with these beautiful, playful children. Let's take a moment to pray together, wind down together, and shower each other with hugs and kisses as our children find rest in the comfort of their parents' love.
- I'm thankful we had meals to eat today. I'm thankful we aren't hungry. Thank You, God, for our house, which keeps us warm and dry. I'm going to set up a recurring donation to the food pantry so people in my community do not go without.

God gave my children so many gifts and talents. I want to show my children how to use their gifts to glorify Him.

In practice, this means eliminating the things from our lives that don't lead us to know, love, and serve God more. If it doesn't give glory to God and doesn't contribute to the family's sanctity, it must be eliminated. That includes TV shows, movies, video games, recreational activities, kids' extracurricular activities, clothing, books, friend groups, food habits, music, sports, Internet usage, phone usage, and so on. These are not bad in and of themselves, but when we spend too much time focusing on any of these, we make them gods, prioritizing them over the one true God, who is all-loving and deserving of all our love.

- If we spend too much time in the evening binge-watching our favorite shows, it will take time away from prayer and spiritual reading.
- If we allow our kids too much TV time, it can pollute their minds with worldly things and makes the Faith less appealing.
- If we spend our entire evenings chauffeuring kids from activity to activity, we will rob our family of precious quality time together, time that could be spent cultivating virtue and strengthening the domestic church.
- If we invest too much time and attention in our kids' activities, we will show them that becoming successful athletes, dancers, and musicians is more important than becoming saints.
- If we waste time on our phones or computers, becoming consumed by current events and social media trends, we will fill our mind with negativity and, again, rob our family of precious time together.

Put God first, no matter what. Is that an extreme idea? Not at all. Taking the necessary steps in your state of life to strengthen your relationship with God and get your family to Heaven is exactly what you are supposed to be doing.

Occasionally watching TV or a movie together is not bad, as long as it's not the default way to spend the evening (and if the show or movie is not filled with vulgarity, promiscuity, or other godless behavior). Some kids' shows are perfectly fine to watch, but in moderation and with supervision. Nowadays, we must be extremely vigilant about the grooming that happens in kids' shows.

Both cell phones and the Internet are inescapable in our technologically dependent society, but we must set boundaries and ensure that their usage is for God's glory. Here again, we need to be aware of the dangers of grooming.

Team sports and other extracurricular activities are wonderful ways to teach children the virtues and help them learn the value of teamwork, cooperation, discipline, consistency, and healthfulness. These activities are tools to serve God and enjoy His creation, but they are not the end goal.

If we orient our lives toward God for the sake of desiring to know, love, and serve Him, we position ourselves to receive the graces necessary to grow in holiness. We have to make the difficult, seemingly impossible, decision to step away from the world to answer our call to sainthood.

Let's be practical

What are five things that are taking too much time and attention away from your faith and family, and what can you focus on instead?

Pro tip

In answering that question, ask for input from your spouse and children, since you are working on growing in holiness together!

Examples:

Instead of ...	try this:
Binging on TV at night with your spouse	Have a date night with prayer and spiritual reading; watch a webisode on Catholic marriage and discuss it together
Participating in traveling sports teams with tournaments on Sundays	Join a different league with games during the week
Spending Sundays watching college or pro sports on TV or the Internet	Visit a park or go hiking with your kids; cook dinner as a family; play a family-friendly game

Instead of ...	try this:
Watching Saturday-morning cartoons	Attend or watch Saturday-morning Mass; watch EWTN kids' Faith Factory shows
Wasting time on your phone, tablet, or computer	Put your phone, tablet, or computer away at certain times during the day; offer up your temptations for your family's holiness

Your turn:

Instead of ...	We will try this ...

Here are other ways we can make God the priority in our daily lives:

It might feel strange to put these down in writing, but we need to identify the distractions in order to overcome them. By replacing the false gods in our lives with properly ordered activities, we will be more able to recognize how little we might love God right now, based on how much time we think of spending with Him.

Put God first, no matter what.

"The secret to freedom is to prefer God to everything and to do everything for God." (Mother Angelica)

6

Prepare for a Total Transformation

When our will is one with God's will, then nothing can happen to us except what God wills; thus, we will never be disappointed.[6]

—Venerable Archbishop Fulton J. Sheen

When it comes to practicing our Catholic Faith, there is no need to reinvent the wheel—and it's a good thing, because what parent has time for that?

Our Catholic Faith has a rich two-thousand-year heritage of teachings, devotions, prayers, and writings. If you make it a priority to commit yourself to practice the Faith in your everyday life, your soul is going to be completely changed. You won't simply be "going through the motions" of being Catholic; through the grace of God, you will come to love your Faith, seek God's will in all things, and be totally transformed for the better.

[6] Archbishop Fulton J. Sheen, *Lord, Teach Us to Pray: A Fulton Sheen Anthology*, comp. Al Smith (Manchester, NH: Sophia Institute Press, 2019), 177.

Dave and I found that, in the process of pursuing holiness for ourselves and our children, we were radically changing the way we lived.

At first, the experience was uncomfortable. We began spending less time with certain friends who didn't have the same orientation toward Heaven. We began listening to other kinds of music and watching other kinds of TV shows—and we watched much less TV.

We began planning our schedule around Mass instead of planning Mass around our schedule.

We began radically restructuring our lives to live our Faith every day, not just on Sundays.

Praying the Rosary together, wearing our scapulars, attending daily Mass, making every moment an opportunity for prayer, taking up spiritual reading, going to Confession regularly, and visiting Jesus in Eucharistic Adoration are now no-brainers to us, and that wasn't always the case.

We still need to perfect our discipline and consistency—after all, we are tired, imperfect parents—but we have a clear road map of what we as tired parents need to do to keep our faith alive. We have made our home a safe haven filled with sacramentals and fortified by the intercession of our family's patron saints. We have clear expectations of what is and what is not allowed in our home. We have the graces of our marriage and the sacraments. We have friends who share our desire for Heaven. We know what we need to get ourselves and our kids to Heaven. We desire to love God.

Finally, we are understanding our Faith more and more deeply. We know that you can grow in your understanding of the Faith too.

Let's be practical

The next part of this book offers concrete ways to start growing in your love of God and getting your family to Heaven. It begins with building a foundation of prayer.

Pro tip

Work through this book as a family and complete the writing portions together. You are growing in holiness together and striving toward Heaven together!

"I can stand tall, not because of any power of my own, but because Your Power is my shield, my weapon, my protection, and my victory." (Mother Angelica)

PART 2

Building a Foundation of Prayer

7

Small Changes Become Big Changes

If you have lost the taste for prayer, you will regain the desire for it by returning humbly to its practice.[7]

—Pope St. Paul VI

When Dave and I began the process of repaying my student-loan debt and building good financial habits, there were certain steps we followed and certain guidelines by which we abided. Every decision we made was oriented toward becoming debt-free. On its own, each decision seemed insignificant, but all those decisions added up and allowed us to change our spending habits, our saving habits, and our outlook on money.

Similarly, in our prayer life, we noticed that the small changes led to big changes over time. At first, it was awkward and clunky praying the Rosary together. It took several tries to get used to wearing the brown scapular. And, initially, we dismissed the idea of

[7] Pope St. Paul VI, apostolic exhortation *Evangelica testificatio* (June 29, 1971), no. 42.

taking three young kids to daily Mass. After all, it was hard enough to get the kids to Mass on Sundays. Why would we willingly subject ourselves to that when there was no obligation?

But the truth is, our excuses were pathetic:

- "We don't have time to pray the Rosary because we need to get the kids to bed."
- "I can't wear the scapular because it will show while I'm at work."
- "I can't wear my scapular because the baby will tug on it while she's nursing."
- "We don't need to worry about taking the kids to daily Mass because they won't pay attention anyway and it will eat up our whole evening."
- "We don't have time to go to daily Mass because we have too much to do at home."
- "It's too hard to get to Confession because I work on Saturdays."
- "There's no way we can each do a holy hour every week."
- "We aren't at a point in our lives where we have the luxury of doing intense spiritual reading." (We are just now starting to attack this excuse, and what a difference it has made!)

The problem with all these excuses is that they're not true. What we lacked was not time or energy but love. Surely, we make time for the things that are important to us—the things we love. And surely, if we want to accomplish something difficult, we're creative enough to find a way.

We didn't think we had time to pray the Rosary, but you bet we had time to binge-watch TV shows at night.

We thought we could justify not wearing the scapular because of minor inconveniences, but we hadn't really tried hard enough.

We didn't think our kids would behave during daily Mass, but we took them to other places where they were expected to behave and follow instructions.

We hadn't fathomed the idea of going to Confession at other parishes, but we had no problem shopping around at various stores for groceries, craft supplies, home renovation tools, or any other items we needed. We also hadn't considered making an appointment for Confession with a local priest, even though we make lots of doctor appointments for our kids and ourselves.

I could go on and on, but I'm sure you get the point. Once we decided that our Faith was truly important to us and that we needed to grow in our love of God, it became easier to make accommodations to put our faith into action.

For us, making excuses was easy. Blaming others was easy. Both were much easier than taking responsibility for our own failings. But it finally occurred to us that, as eating healthfully and exercising are at the service of our bodies, the Mass, the sacraments, sacramentals, and daily prayer are at the service of our souls. Dave and I knew that if we were going to say that we are Catholic, we had to act like it. We had to live it. We had to make daily choices to love God, serve Him, and help our children do the same.

Let's be practical

The following ten chapters offer "beginner" ways to jump-start the practice of your Catholic Faith in your daily life.

Pro tip

God desires our faithfulness and knows we can do nothing without Him. Remember to commit to loving God above all and asking for the grace to build a firm foundation of prayer.

"If you want to do something for the Lord, do it! Whatever you feel needs to be done, even though you're shaking in your boots and you're scared to death, take the first step." (Mother Angelica)

8

House Blessing and Enthronement of the Most Sacred Heart of Jesus

He promised me that all those who are devoted and consecrated to Him will never be lost. Since He is the source of all blessings, He will shower them in abundance on every place where a picture of His divine Heart shall be set up and honored. He will reunite broken families, will protect and help those who are in any necessity and those who approach Him with confidence.[8]

—St. Margaret Mary Alacoque

Perhaps there's no better way to begin revamping and reorienting your spiritual life than by having your house blessed and by enthroning Jesus as King of your hearts, your home, and your family.

The family is the domestic church, the place in which your children will learn the most about their Faith. It is in your home

[8] *The Letters of St. Margaret Mary Alacoque: Apostle of the Sacred Heart* (Charlotte, NC: TAN Books, 2012), Letter 36, 50.

that your children will see God's love firsthand through their parents. It is where they should learn their prayers, grow in virtue, and experience the power of forgiveness.

It should also be a place where they see their Faith in action at all times. What they see, hear, and do in the home growing up will carry into their adulthood. And if they don't learn the truths of the Faith at home, it's guaranteed they won't learn it from the secular world.

Having your home blessed is a means by which you can drive away any evil that might reside in your home, offer spiritual protection to your children, and provide an outward sign for your children and yourselves that your home is a holy place where the Lord resides.

The same goes for enthroning the Sacred Heart of Jesus in your home. Not only are there graces bestowed on those who honor Jesus in this way, but the enthronement also serves as an outward sign of your family's commitment to living the Faith and loving the Lord.

There are a variety of forms of house blessings, which can be done by a priest or a deacon.

An added benefit of having your house blessed is the opportunity to welcome your pastor into your home if you've not done so already. Invite Father over for dinner or coffee and dessert, and ensure that the kids are present. Father will lead you from room to room, blessing your abode with holy water. Your children will see the holy water sprinkled upon every part of your home. You'll be able to explain to them that your home is a special place where God is present, as well as a place where the family grows in love for God and for one another.

Did you know that Jesus promised twelve special graces to those who have a devotion to His Sacred Heart?

The twelve promises of the Sacred Heart of Jesus are these:

1. I will give them all the graces necessary in their state of life.
2. I will establish peace in their homes.
3. I will comfort them in all their afflictions.
4. I will be their secure refuge during life and, above all, in death.
5. I will bestow abundant blessings upon all their undertakings.
6. Sinners will find in my Heart the source and infinite ocean of mercy.
7. Lukewarm souls shall become fervent.
8. Fervent souls shall quickly mount to high perfection.
9. I will bless every place in which an image of my Heart is exposed and honored.
10. I will give to priests the gift of touching the most hardened hearts.
11. Those who shall promote this devotion shall have their names written in my Heart.
12. I promise you in the excessive mercy of my Heart that my all-powerful love will grant to all those who receive Holy Communion on the First Fridays in nine consecutive months the grace of final perseverance; they shall not die in my disgrace, nor without receiving the sacraments. My divine Heart shall be their safe refuge in this last moment.

Jesus wishes to bestow these graces upon you, if you will accept them and commit to honoring Him as King of your life.

The Sacred Heart Enthronement Network has all the resources your family needs to prepare to enthrone Jesus as King of your home. They even offer eight-by-ten-inch images of the Sacred Heart of Jesus and Immaculate Heart of Mary. You can get the enthronement preparation kit at WelcomeHisHeart.com.

Let's be practical

Schedule a time for your parish priest to bless your home. Complete the enthronement preparation and enthrone Jesus as King of your home and family.

Pro tip

Make a habit of inviting your priest over to bless your home on or around the anniversary of your first house blessing. On the anniversary of your enthronement and on the feast of the Sacred Heart of Jesus (which is a movable feast, the first Friday after the solemnity of Corpus Christi), renew your commitment to honor Jesus as King of your home.

Date of House Blessing	Date of Sacred Heart Enthronement

"When you have Jesus, what have you to fear?" (Mother Angelica)

9

Consecration to the Blessed Mother and St. Joseph

Let us love Jesus above all, let us love Mary as our mother; but then, how could we keep from loving Joseph, who was so intimately united to both Jesus and Mary? And how can we honor him better than by imitating his virtues? Now, what else did he do in all his life but contemplate, study, and adore Jesus, even in the midst of his daily labors? Behold, therefore, our model.[9]

—St. Madeleine Sophie Barat

If Dave and I were left on our own to try to get our kids to Heaven, our poor babies wouldn't have a prayer. But now that we've consecrated our entire family to Jesus through Mary and St. Joseph, we know that the Blessed Mother and the foster father of Jesus are

[9] Quoted in Donald H. Calloway, M.I.C., *Consecration to St. Joseph: The Wonders of Our Spiritual Father* (Stockbridge, MA: Marian Press, 2019), Day 2.

in Heaven praying for and protecting our children and watching over us as we raise our children on earth.

When we consecrate ourselves and our families to Mary and St. Joseph, we are in no way diminishing our love for God, nor are we intending to love them more than we love Jesus. In fact, it is quite the opposite. Through Mary, we learn to be more like Jesus. Through her motherly and Immaculate Heart, we see her Son the way she sees Him, and we learn to love Him as she loves Him. Mary—immaculate, perfect, sinless, and blameless—would never insist that we love her more than we love Jesus. In her perfection, humility, and grace, she leads us to Jesus.

The same goes for St. Joseph. This humble, just, righteous man, who obeyed the law and was faithful to God's will for his life, would never insist that he is more worthy of our attention than Jesus is. By consecrating ourselves to St. Joseph, we ask him to adopt us spiritually into the Holy Family so that we may experience his comfort and protection. As he raised Jesus in faith and virtue, guarded Him from harm, and stayed faithful to his earthly duties as a carpenter, St. Joseph desires to be our spiritual father and protector and a model for our everyday lives on earth.

A consecration is a way of pledging to love Jesus more perfectly with the help of the Blessed Mother and St. Joseph. At a time when the family is under attack, we parents need to seek the guidance and protection of the Holy Spouses, the Blessed Mother and St. Joseph.

Before a consecration, there is usually a thirty-three-day preparation period involving catechesis and praying specifically for the intention of being evermore devoted to Jesus through Mary and St. Joseph. With proper planning, the consecration day will fall on a feast day of Mary or St. Joseph, or both: the Annunciation, the Nativity of the Lord, the Nativity of Mary, the Immaculate Conception, the Assumption, St. Joseph, St. Joseph the Worker, Mary the Mother of God, or another such feast.

EWTN Religious Catalogue (ewtnRC.com) offers several versions of the total consecration to Jesus through Mary (by St. Louis Marie de Montfort); two consecrations to St. Joseph (one by Fr. Donald Calloway, one by Devin Schadt); and several Marian consecrations for children. Pick any of these and do not hesitate to begin your preparation. You will be amazed at the outpouring of graces God will bestow on your family!

To Jesus, through Mary and St. Joseph!

Let's be practical

Complete the preparation for the total consecration to Jesus through Mary, and then pray the prayer of consecration as a family. Do the same with the consecration to St. Joseph.

Pro tip

Renew your consecrations to Jesus through Mary and to St. Joseph every year on the anniversary of your original consecration. And if you have friends who have not yet consecrated themselves to Mary and St. Joseph, pass along your books to them and encourage them to do so!

Date of Consecration to the Blessed Mother	Date of Consecration to St. Joseph

"Renew within us all a greater love for Mary our Mother, and let her example of faith, hope, and love spur us on to great things." (Mother Angelica)

10

Holy Reminders

You know, I wear a crucifix because I don't want to forget that God is with me. I like to hold on to Him when things get difficult, because it reminds me how much Jesus loves me. He loved me this much. And He wants me to understand that in this position, in this intolerable, painful position, He forgave. That's what it means to be saintly.

—Mother Angelica

In the six years I co-hosted *EWTN Religious Catalogue*, I can't count the number of times I said the words "holy reminders." It's the term Mother Angelica used on the show to describe the sacramentals, books, artwork, and statues that remind us of our Faith and call us to prayer. What a perfect term!

I firmly believe that every family should have every single one of the following items:

- Divine Mercy image
- St. Benedict Medals
- rosaries
- Brown Scapulars
- Miraculous Medals
- holy-water fonts
- crucifixes
- statues and images of the Blessed Mother

I say this not to boost sales for *EWTN Religious Catalogue* but because every one of these items, when blessed, will offer spiritual protection; will draw you to prayer; will invite guests and visitors to reflect; and will remind you of your ultimate goal in life: to get yourself and your family to Heaven. Dave and I have seen how, by filling our house with holy reminders, our home has truly become a sacred place, a domestic church.

When I look at the Sacred Heart and Immaculate Heart portraits above our fireplace, I contemplate how we've invited Jesus and His Queen Mother to reign in our home and that our mantel is their throne. Those who know us know that the fireplace is what made us fall in love with our home and the number-one reason we put in an offer to buy it! Neighbors who walk by our house can see Jesus and Mary when they look in the window, and anyone who comes to our front door is immediately greeted by the King and Queen. It is in front of the images of the Sacred and Immaculate Hearts that Dave and I can reconcile with each other, work out disputes, and make reparation for our sins, together. It's hard to keep fighting when you're face-to-face with the Two Hearts!

While I wash dishes, I gaze at the simple crucifix above the sink and offer my chores for my family's salvation. I also occasionally gripe to Jesus about how my day is faring, and He helps put things in perspective.

When we tuck in our children at night, we see the Sacred Heart and Miraculous Medals above their beds and ask Jesus and Mary to watch over our babies as they sleep.

When my children are playing, my eye catches the picture of the Visitation above them. It's one of my favorite holy reminders in our home. It reminds me to pray for my oldest child's godmother.

When I see a certain old prayer card of St. Thérèse, I pray for a wayward family member whom I've been praying for every day for years.

When I sit at the table to do homeschool lessons with my kids, I see my childhood rosary hanging from a portrait of the Holy Family. The glass beads were shattered and the crucifix was mangled in a car accident when I was sixteen—a car accident that nearly killed me—and I'm reminded of my guardian angel and of the fact that God isn't finished with me here yet.

And while I'm at the kitchen table, I also gaze at our picture of St. Anthony of Padua and the Child Jesus. Our children regularly turn to this image of St. Anthony for help in finding lost items, but I'm constantly reminded of the prayer I prayed over and over when a pregnancy complication threatened our son's life: "Please, St. Anthony, don't let us lose our baby boy!"

What we display in our homes says a lot about who we are, whom we love, and what we treasure. Surrounding ourselves with holy reminders is one of the best ways to grow in our love of God by seeing Him in sacred art, calling on Him in prayer, and disposing our hearts to receive graces in the sacraments and to be docile to His will.

Following are brief explanations of the must-have holy reminders for your home. They are available at Catholic bookstores and websites everywhere, though we'll always be partial to the beautiful, high-quality holy reminders on *EWTN Religious Catalogue*.

Divine Mercy Image

> My daughter, know that My Heart is mercy itself. From this sea of mercy graces flow out upon the whole world.... I have opened My Heart as a living fountain of mercy. Let all souls draw life from it. (Jesus to St. Faustina)[10]

[10] *Divine Mercy in My Soul: The Diary of Saint Maria Faustina Kowalska* [hereafter "*Diary*"], nos. 1777 and 1520.

Relative to the two-thousand-year history of the Church, the Divine Mercy devotion is fairly new. Jesus Himself gave the message of His Divine Mercy to St. Faustina Kowalska in the 1930s. However, God's plan for the salvation of the world was always a plan for mercy.

In 1931, Jesus appeared to St. Faustina in a vision. He was wearing a white garment and had two rays coming from His Heart: a red ray that symbolized blood and a pale ray that symbolized water—the blood and water that gushed from His Heart on the Cross when the centurion lanced His side.

Jesus told St. Faustina,

> Paint an image according to the pattern you see, with the signature: Jesus, I trust in You. I promise that the soul that will venerate this image will not perish. I also promise victory over [its] enemies already here on earth, especially at the hour of death. I Myself will defend it as My own glory.[11]

> I am offering people a vessel with which they are to keep coming for graces to the fountain of mercy. That vessel is this image with the signature: Jesus, I trust in You.[12]

> I desire that this image be venerated, first in your chapel, and [then] throughout the world.[13]

Jesus Himself wants you to venerate the image of His Divine Mercy. That should be reason enough to display this image in your home!

[11] *Diary*, nos. 47, 48.
[12] *Diary*, no. 327.
[13] *Diary*, no. 47.

The Divine Mercy image is more than a decoration: it's a devotion and a reminder of our need for God's mercy and love. If we think we love our kids infinitely, imagine how much more God loves them!

When you pass this image in your home, you can pray a short passing prayer:

> Jesus, I trust in You.
>
> Jesus, have mercy on me.
>
> O Blood and Water, which gushed forth from the Heart of Jesus as a font of Mercy for us, I trust in You![14]

Or any variation of these.

When you pray the Chaplet of Divine Mercy together as a family, you can gaze upon Jesus and contemplate His abundant love and mercy.

St. Benedict Medal

> We must ... prepare our hearts and bodies for battle of holy obedience to His instructions. What is not possible to us by nature, let us ask the Lord to supply by the help of His grace. (St. Benedict of Nursia)[15]

For a powerhouse sacramental that can drive away evil, go with the St. Benedict jubilee medal or the St. Benedict Crucifix, which includes the medal. We have St. Benedict Medals and Crucifixes all over our home and in our car.

[14] *Diary*, no. 187.

[15] Rule of St. Benedict, prologue, from *RB 1980: The Rule of St. Benedict in English* (Collegeville, MN: Liturgical Press, 1981), 18.

It should be very clearly stated that Catholics do not believe that the St. Benedict Medal, or any sacramental, is a good luck-charm or a magical token. Catholics are not superstitious, and we don't play around with such dangerous articles.

The *Catechism of the Catholic Church* says that sacramentals are "sacred signs instituted by the Church" that prepare us "to receive the fruit of the sacraments and sanctify different circumstances of life" (CCC 1677).

The St. Benedict Medal is special. St. Benedict is known as the Father of Western Monasticism and is one of the patron saints of Europe because of his remarkable influence in spreading Christianity. In Jesus' name, he performed many miracles. Over the centuries, St. Benedict has been invoked for protection against the tricks of the devil. This medal not only symbolizes his life and mission but also contains a prayer of exorcism:

> *Vade retro Satana! Nunquam suade mihi vana! Sunt mala quae libas. Ipse venena bibas!* (Begone Satan! Never tempt me with your vanities! What you offer me is evil. Drink the poison yourself!)

The medal need not be worn in any specific way. It is commonly worn on a chain around the neck but can also be hung on a wall, placed on a key ring or a bracelet, or attached to a Brown Scapular or a rosary.

When we wear it or display it in our home, we are reminded to pray for spiritual protection, for defense against impure thoughts, for strength to reject temptation, and for courage to, as St. Benedict taught, "Walk in God's ways, with the Gospel as our guide."[16]

[16] *Rule of St. Benedict*, prologue.

Rosaries — Everywhere

> If you say the Holy Rosary every day, with a spirit of faith and love, Our Lady will make sure she leads you very far along her Son's path. (St. Josemaría Escrivá)[17]

I don't say this to be funny, or even to speak in hyperbole, but there should be multiple rosaries in every room of your home. My guess is that they're the most ubiquitous sacramental of all time. At one point, Dave, who is a convert to the Faith, had more rosaries than I had.

I wish people truly understood the power of the Holy Rosary. Like the St. Benedict Medal, a rosary is not a charm. It is a sacramental through which we can worship Jesus, implore the help of His Mother, and transform our hearts to grow in love of God.

Since there are so many occasions on which we receive rosaries as gifts, it makes sense for a Catholic family to have many. Please, don't leave them in a drawer. Place them on nightstands and end tables, hang them on photo frames, stow several in your car, and hang them on hooks above your prayer table or atop your office desk. Keep them within reach so you can always be ready to meditate on the life of Our Lord through the lens of His Mother.

Here's what some of the holy members of the Church have said about the Holy Rosary:

> Say your rosary every day, either alone or with others, and as you recite it accustom yourself to meditate affectionately

[17] *Furrow*, no. 691, Josemaría Escrivá, https://www.escrivaworks.org/book/furrow-point-691.htm.

on the mysteries of Our Savior and of His holy Mother. This is the easiest and frequently the most fruitful of all mediations. (St. Francis de Sales)[18]

Never will anyone who says his Rosary every day ... be led astray. This is a statement that I would gladly sign with my blood. (St. Louis Marie de Montfort)[19]

One day, through the Rosary and the Scapular, Our Lady will save the world. (St. Dominic)[20]

The Rosary is a long chain that links heaven and earth. One end of it is in our hands and the other end is in the hands of the Holy Virgin.... The Rosary prayer rises like incense to the feet of the Almighty. (St. Thérèse of Lisieux)[21]

It is our ardent wish that this devotion shall be restored to the place of honor; in the city and in the village, in the family and in the workshop, in the noble's house and in the peasant's; that it should be to all a dear devotion and

[18] St. Francis de Sales, *The Saint Francis de Sales Collection* (London: Catholic Way Publishing, 2015), *The Secret of Sanctity*, pt. 1, chap. 1, "The Regulation of Our Actions."

[19] Quoted in Donald H. Calloway, M.I.C., *26 Champions of the Rosary: The Essential Guide to the Greatest Heroes of the Rosary* (Stockbridge, MA: Marian Press, 2017), "St. Louis de Montfort."

[20] Quoted in John M. Haffert, *The Sign of Her Heart*, quoted in "The Scapular," Catholic Tradition, http://www.catholictradition.org/Mary/dominics-prophecy.htm.

[21] Quoted on the website of the Society of the Little Flower, https://www.littleflower.org/st-therese-rosary/.

> a noble sign of their faith; that it may be a sure way to the gaining of the favor of pardon. (Pope St. Leo XIII)[22]
>
> The holy Rosary is a powerful weapon. Use it with confidence and you'll be amazed at the results. (St. Josemaría Escrivá)[23]
>
> Pray the Rosary frequently. It costs so little, and it's worth so much! (St. Padre Pio)
>
> Since we all need to pray, God asks of us, as a kind of daily installment, a prayer which is within our reach: the Rosary, which can be recited either in common or in private, either in Church or in the presence of the Blessed Sacrament, or at home, either with the rest of the family or alone, either when travelling or while walking quietly in the fields. A mother of a family can say the Rosary while she rocks her baby's cradle or does the housework. Our day has twenty-four hours in it. It is not asking a great deal to set aside a quarter of an hour for the spiritual life, for our intimate and familiar converse with God. (Sr. Lucia of Fatima)[24]

I could offer dozens more quotes. But I should add that it's not enough simply to possess rosaries. You have to *use* them! They're not decorations but devotions.

[22] Pope St. Leo XIII, encyclical *Iucunda semper expectatione* (September 8, 1894), no. 9.

[23] St. Josemaría Escrivá, The Way, no. 558, Josemaría Escrivá, https://www.escrivaworks.org/book/the_way-point-558.htm.

[24] Sr. Lucia of Jesus and of the Immaculate Heart, quoted in World Apostolate of Fatima, *Spiritual Guide for the Salvation of Souls and World Peace* (Washington, NJ: World Apostolate of Fatima, USA/ Blue Army, 2008), 535.

And listen, it's hard. At the end of the day, you're tired. The kids are tired. You're trying to get the house cleaned up and get the little ones to bed. There's yelling. There's chaos. There's laundry everywhere. How in the world are you going to get everyone settled to pray the Rosary together?

This is one of those areas in which Dave and I used to fall into making excuses for not praying the Rosary every single day, even though Our Lady of Fatima specifically requested it ("Pray the Rosary every day to obtain peace for the world" [May 13, 1917]).

The Rosary takes only twenty to twenty-five minutes to pray. And those will be some of the most valuable minutes of your day. Lovingly, I'm telling you to stop making excuses and start praying the Rosary! I don't have all the answers, but here are a few suggestions to make praying the Rosary as a family more feasible and enjoyable:

- Don't expect any child under six years old to be able to pray the Rosary in its entirety consistently and devoutly. Not many adults can focus entirely on the Rosary either.
- Don't wait until the end of the day to pray. Pray at a time when the kids are fed, rested, and docile.
- Let your children pick the rosary beads they want to use during prayer. While they are young, ensure that there is a selection of durable rosaries. Our son went through a phase of pulling rosaries apart, and I'm sure he's not the only child who has done that!
- Invite your children to lead a decade or two, as they are able. Children ages three to six often enjoy being leaders and exercising their knowledge. Praise any efforts at leading, as this is an early sign that they are building a relationship with Jesus and Mary.

- Sometimes it will be just you and your spouse praying together. If the kids aren't in great moods, ask their guardian angels to pray with you.
- Pray in the car together, especially heading to or from Mass. If your drive is less than twenty minutes, stay in the car until you finish the Rosary. If your drive is short, pray part of the Rosary on the way to Mass and the rest on the way home.
- Set a time to pray and stick to it.
- Pray half the Rosary in the morning and half in the evening.
- If you miss praying the Rosary one day, don't get discouraged, but get right back to praying the next day.

Whatever you need to do, do it. Here is more great advice from the saints:

> You always leave the Rosary for later, and you end up not saying it at all because you are sleepy. If there is no other time, say it in the street without letting anybody notice it. It will, moreover, help you to have presence of God. (St. Josemaría Escrivá)[25]

> In times of darkness, holding the Rosary is like holding our Blessed Mother's Hand. (St. Padre Pio)[26]

[25] *Furrow*, no. 478.

[26] Quoted on the website of the National Centre for Padre Pio, Barto, Pennsylvania, https://www.padrepio.org/pray/how-to-pray-the-rosary/.

Brown Scapular and Miraculous Medal

> No sinner need ever fear that he shall be rejected by Mary, if he has recourse to her mercy; and as such, desires to save the most miserable. (St. Alphonsus Liguori)[27]

If you're not enrolled in the Brown Scapular, or if you're not wearing it faithfully, you're missing out on a beautiful gift from the Blessed Mother. In 1251, Our Lady appeared to St. Simon Stock, a Carmelite, and gave him the Brown Scapular. She asked that the faithful wear a brown, wool scapular around their necks as a sign of devotion, trust, and confidence in her. And to those who do so, she promises:

> Whosoever dies invested with this scapular shall be preserved from the eternal flames. It is a sign of salvation, a sure safeguard in danger, a pledge of peace and of my special protection until the end of the ages.[28]

I suggest going to SistersofCarmel.com for more information on the Brown Scapular and for details on how to be invested, or enrolled, in it. You'll also learn about the Sabbatine Privilege, which carries certain conditions that must be fulfilled (but are not impossible, even for tired parents).

As tired parents, we should all be jumping on this devotion. The Blessed Mother so graciously offers us a surefire means of salvation, and if we do as she asks out of love for her and for her Son, she has promised to protect us from the fires of Hell. If it

[27] St. Alphonsus Liguori, *The Glories of Mary*, chap. 2, "Vita, Dulcedo," sect. 1, Kindle ed.

[28] "Why Do We Celebrate the Feast of Our Lady of Mount Carmel?" EWTN, https://www.ewtn.com/catholicism/seasons-and-feast-days/our-lady-of-mount-carmel-21181.

sounds too good to be true, consider that the entirety of God's love for us seems too good to be true. But it is true, and God created us out of love to be with Him in Heaven forever. This is what we are made for!

The Blessed Mother has also gifted humanity with the Miraculous Medal, one of the most widely recognized devotional items of our Faith.

In 1830, she appeared to St. Catherine Labouré and requested that a medal be created bearing the image she revealed and the prayer "O Mary, conceived without sin, pray for us who have recourse to thee." She promised:

> Have a medal struck upon this model. Those who wear it will receive great graces, especially if they wear it around the neck. Those who repeat this prayer with devotion will be, in a special manner, under the protection of the Mother of God. Graces will be abundantly bestowed upon those who have confidence.[29]

There's an interesting point to make about the Miraculous Medal. At one point, St. Catherine asked the Blessed Mother why, in the image on the medal, some of the rays that extend from Mary's hands do not reach the earth. Mary responded, "Those are the graces for which people forget to ask."[30] The graces to be good, holy parents are freely available to us, but we must ask for them with humility and trust!

[29] "St. Catherine and the Miraculous Medal," Daughters of Charity, https://www.daughtersofcharity.com/who-we-are/miraculous-medal/.

[30] "Origins," Our Lady of the Miraculous Medal, https://www.ourladyofmm.com/html/origins.html.

When we put on our Brown Scapulars and our Miraculous Medals, there are several short prayers we can pray:

> Mary, Mother of Jesus, be my mother too.
>
> Mary, help me be a good mother, like you.
>
> O Mary, conceived without sin, pray for us who have recourse to thee.
>
> O Jesus, through the Immaculate Heart of Mary, I offer You all my prayers, works, joys, and sufferings of this day.
>
> Mary, I am totally yours. I entrust my entire day to you. May all I do be for love of your Son, Jesus.

Or any variation of these.

There have been entire books written about the Brown Scapular and the Miraculous Medal; there's no way I could do justice to either with so little space here. If you're a tired parent and you want to receive the graces to grow in holiness and to help your family do the same, please wear the Brown Scapular and the Miraculous Medal!

Holy-Water Fonts

> From long experience I have learned that there is nothing like holy water to put devils to flight and prevent them from coming back. (St. Teresa of Ávila)[31]

While hosting *EWTN Religious Catalogue*, I frequently told viewers that holy reminders are made to be used. A great example is a holy-water font.

[31] Quoted in Rev. Henry Theiler, S.O.Cist., *Holy Water and Its Significance for Catholics* (Manchester, NH: Sophia Institute Press, 2016), 47.

Whereas Catholics are familiar with holy-water fonts at the entrances of churches, fewer are familiar with the practice of having holy-water fonts in homes—and not just a single holy-water font but even one in every room!

Holy water reminds us of our Baptism. When we use it while making the Sign of the Cross, it is a call to prayer.

But wait, there's more! Holy water also offers protection from evil. In fact, when a priest blesses the water that becomes holy water, he prays prayers of exorcism.

"Holy water has a special power to defend us against all attacks of the devil," Pope Pius IX tells us. "When we make the Sign of the Cross with holy water, we gain each time an indulgence."[32] To receive this partial indulgence—that is, the remission of some of the temporal punishment due to sins that have been forgiven—we must make the Sign of the Cross with holy water while praying, "In the name of the Father, and of the Son, and of the Holy Spirit. Amen"; and we must be detached from sin and in a state of grace.

You can see why this is an important holy reminder to have in your home and to use often. Bless yourselves and your children when you wake up, throughout the day, when you're praying together, and before going to bed. You can pray any short prayer you'd like, but pray it out loud:

> In the name of the Father, and of the Son, and of the Holy Spirit. Amen. Lord, by this water and by Your Precious Blood, wash away my sins. Amen.

[32] Francis Spirago, *The Catechism Explained: An Exhaustive Exposition of the Christian Religion*, ed. Richard Frederick Clarke (New York: Benziger Brothers, 1899), 107.

Thou shalt sprinkle me, O Lord, with hyssop, and I shall be cleansed. Thou shalt wash me, and I shall become whiter than snow. (from the Asperges Me)

Lord, with this holy water purify me.

Dave and I have discovered that holy water is effective during kids' temper tantrums. We are not suggesting that our kids need to be exorcised, but the act of stepping back and intentionally blessing our kids gives them a chance to breathe and relax. All the kids gather around, I pour some holy water from the bottle into their hands, and while they're making the Sign of the Cross, they giggle as the holy water dribbles down their faces. Parents can pray for peace and calm, asking for the grace to handle the situation in the best way.

At ewtnRC.com, you can purchase a variety of beautiful fonts and bottles for storing holy water. Fill the bottles with holy water from your church (either directly from the baptismal font or from the special holy-water receptacle, usually in the narthex or the atrium) and keep them in your car, in your purse, and throughout your home.

I once saw a respected Catholic Instagram influencer show off "holy water spray bottles." She used colorful plastic spray bottles from the dollar store, filled them with holy water, and made "Holy Water" labels with masking tape. Then she proceeded to laugh about squirting her kids with holy water. Please do not do this. Holy water is a sacramental, and although we might sometimes joke about needing to douse our kids with holy water, we still should respect it for what it is and what it does.

A Crucifix in Every Room

O souls that seek to walk in security and comfort in spiritual things! If you did but know how necessary it is to suffer

> and to endure in order to reach this security! (St. John of the Cross)[33]

Throughout the centuries, the saints have told us, again and again, that if we want to love Jesus, we must also love the Cross. If we want to grow in holiness, we must be willing to endure trials, to bear our sufferings patiently, to pick up our crosses daily. To the rest of the ancient pagan world, the cross was a tool for a long, painful, humiliating public execution. To the modern pagan world, the cross has stigmas too. But we Catholics know that the Cross symbolizes victory over death, triumph over evil, and our salvation.

The Cross is a source of strength in marriage and in family life in which, united with Christ, we are given the grace to overcome hardships and experience the joy of the Resurrection. The Cross is a symbol of new life. Even the crucifix, with the battered body of Our Lord, is a sign of hope and life for us. It is also a powerful reminder of God's infinite love for each one of us.

For this reason, and for the following ones, have a crucifix in each room:

- It is a reminder of our Christian heritage.
- It is a call to prayer every time we see it.
- When we're not sure what to say in prayer, we can simply gaze at our crucified Lord.
- The crucifix represents the unfathomable love and mercy of God in sending His only Son to die for our sins.

[33] *The Living Flame of Love* 2, 28, quoted in *Divine Intimacy* (Virginia Beach, VA: Baronius Press, 2021), no. 132, "Love of the Cross."

- It is a daily reminder to unite our sufferings with Christ's.
- It is a sign for everyone who enters our house that our Faith is inseparable from our everyday lives.

St. John Vianney would add, "Never let your home be without a crucifix upon its walls, to the end that all who enter it may know that you are a disciple of the Crucified Lord, and that you are not ashamed to own it."[34]

There's no need to go out and buy half a dozen crucifixes at once, especially if your monthly budget doesn't allow for it. We have enjoyed receiving them as gifts over the years—one as a wedding gift, two as gifts to welcome new babies, one from a dear friend who brought it back from a trip, and several others from family and friends.

We pray that crucifixes will forever be a great reminder of God's love for you and your family. Let us rejoice in our sufferings and rejoice in God's mercies!

Statues and Images of the Blessed Mother

> Let us be led more and more perfectly by the Immaculata, in any place and in any way she wants to take us, so that, by fulfilling our duties well, we may help to ensure that all souls are won over to her love. (St. Maximilian Kolbe)[35]

I wanted to do a quick inventory of the number of statues and images of the Blessed Mother we have around our house. In our kitchen and living room alone, we have fifteen depictions of Mary

[34] *Thoughts of the Curé D'Ars* (Rockford, IL: TAN Books, 1984).

[35] *The Writings of St. Maximilian Maria Kolbe*, vol. 1, *Letters* (Lugano: Nerbini International, 2017), "Attachment to His Natural Family and the Religious Order to Which He Belonged."

(not including the dozen rosaries hanging in the living room). I stopped counting all the statues, portraits, displayed holy cards, stationery, and medals because I think that having fifteen items in just two rooms of our home illustrates the point.

Too much? St. Maximilian Kolbe wouldn't think so! You see, we love the Blessed Mother dearly. We want to love her more and learn how to love Jesus better. These holy reminders assist us in doing just that. Our Blessed Mother was the first disciple, the first to receive the news of the Incarnation, and the first to be in Jesus' presence. She loved Him more than anyone else on earth. Because of this, she is the perfect role model for all Christians. Mary exercised impeccable humility, obedience, patience, purity, charity, and prayerfulness.

> The greatest saints, those richest in grace and virtue, will be the most assiduous in praying to the most Blessed Virgin, looking up to her as the perfect model to imitate and as a powerful helper to assist them. (St. Louis Marie de Montfort)[36]

When we see these images of Mary, under her many titles, we also are reminded of the way she has interceded for humanity throughout history. Our Blessed Mother has appeared as Our Lady of Fatima, Our Lady of Mount Carmel, Our Lady of Knock, Our Lady of Kibeho, Our Lady of Lourdes, Our Lady of Guadalupe, Our Lady of Victory (also known as Our Lady of the Rosary), and under many other titles.

Mary never points to herself. She always points us to Jesus and is ready to intercede for us. Let us not forget to ask her for her help!

When you pass an image of Mary in your home, you can say any short prayer, such as the Memorare, the Hail Mary, or any variation of these:

[36] *True Devotion to Mary*, no. 46.

Mama Mary, be a mother to me.

Dear Mother, show me how to love Jesus as you did.

Blessed Mother, I bear this [inconvenience, annoyance, frustration, etc.] for love of you and Jesus.

Mary, I'm struggling today. Show me how to be [patient, generous, humble, grateful, joyful, etc.].

Mama Mary, cover me with your protective mantle.

Mother Mary, protect my children and show them the way to your Son.

As with the holy reminders mentioned above, you can bring them into your home piece by piece. Consider asking for them as gifts for birthdays, anniversaries, Christmas, Baptisms, Mother's Day, Father's Day, patron saints' feast days, or "just because."

Mama Mary, always watch over us! Amen.

Catholic Books and Other Spiritual Reading

> Don't neglect your spiritual reading—Reading has made many saints. (St. Josemaría Escrivá)[37]

When was the last time you picked up a solid Catholic book besides this one?

Over the centuries, the saints have produced myriad solid writings through which we can grow in knowledge and understanding. But those writings won't do us much good if we don't read them!

[37] St. Josemaría Escrivá, *The Way*, no. 116, Josemaría Escrivá, https://www.escrivaworks.org/book/the_way-point-116.htm.

Dave and I were guilty of making excuses for not devoting time to spiritual reading, but what ridiculous excuses those were! We had a bad habit of binge-watching old TV shows. We wasted time on *Star Trek* that we could have spent becoming saints. Captain Janeway is great, but she pales in comparison with the real-life examples of St. Thérèse, St. Teresa, St. Edith Stein, St. Monica, and many others.

Since your home is a domestic church, it would be helpful to start a small library of sound Catholic writings, tried-and-true works that have made many saints over the centuries.

It's too hard to pick favorites, but here are ten of the Cowdens' top picks to get you started:

1. Anything by Mother Angelica
2. *The Diary* of St. Faustina
3. *The Story of a Soul* by St. Thérèse of Lisieux
4. *Introduction to the Devout Life* by St. Francis de Sales
5. *The Interior Castle* by St. Teresa of Ávila
6. *The Letters of St. Margaret Mary Alacoque*
7. *The Spiritual Exercises of St. Ignatius of Loyola*
8. *Witness to Hope* (about Pope St. John Paul II) by George Weigel
9. *Three to Get Married* by Ven. Archbishop Fulton J. Sheen
10. A solid Catholic Bible (Revised Standard Version Catholic Edition, Douay-Rheims, or the Jerusalem Bible)

You can trust anything by Ven. Archbishop Fulton J. Sheen, Scott Hahn, or Peter Kreeft and any of the books at ewtnRC.com, which have been reviewed by EWTN's Theology Department for faithfulness to Church teaching. The site also offers a collection of trusted Catholic children's books.

There's no need to amass a huge collection of books, though that might be a temptation. Start with just a few, and take the time to enjoy reading them. Fill your mind with the truths of our Faith, the wisdom of the saints, and the encouragement to pursue sanctity for yourself and your family!

Holy Reminders in the Car and the Workplace

> Are you a handicraftsman? As you sit at work, sing psalms. Do you not wish to sing with your mouth? Do this in your heart; a psalm is a great companion. In this case you shall undergo nothing serious, but shall be able to sit in your workshop as in a monastery. (St. John Chrysostom)[38]

As we strive to grow in love of God and get our family to Heaven, we begin to see our entire lives transformed in the process. We begin to delight in the newfound moments of prayer and refuge. We also see how this brings us closer together as a family.

It starts to make sense to have holy reminders in your car and your workplace because you are used to surrounding yourself in prayer at home.

Keep rosaries, holy water, prayer cards, a prayer book, faith-related audio or music, and saint medals in your car. Don't have them there

[38] St. John Chrysostom, *Homily on Instructions to Catechumens*, Second Instruction, no. 4 in *Nicene and Post-Nicene Fathers*, First Series, vol. 9, trans. T. P. Brandram, ed. Philip Schaff (Buffalo, NY: Christian Literature Publishing, 1889), revised and edited for New Advent by Kevin Knight, http://www.newadvent.org/fathers/1908.htm.

just for the sake of having them there. Use them! Pray the Rosary or the Chaplet of Divine Mercy while you are driving. Even if you cannot finish during your drive, you've still done more than if you hadn't prayed at all.

Not only that, but we can recognize pockets of time God gives us to spend in prayer at work, such as during our commute, on our lunch break, and while running errands. You might find additional time for prayer, depending on your occupation.

Understandably, there are certain limitations to having holy reminders in your workplace. A surgeon can't display religious icons in the operating room; factory workers might be prohibited from wearing jewelry for safety reasons; people in the service and hospitality industries don't necessarily have desks on which to set Catholic books. Obviously, practicality and safety must be considered and taken seriously.

There certainly are creative ways to make prayer part of your workday. These can be small ways, such as taping an image of the Blessed Mother in your locker or keeping your rosary in your pocket. If you have a desk job, you can keep a bottle of holy water in your drawer and bless yourself at the beginning and the end of the workday. You can keep a list of prayer requests at your desk or in your pocket, offering your work for those intentions.

If you have short breaks in your workday, you can take a few minutes to pray the Chaplet of Divine Mercy. When spoken slowly and reverently, it takes only five to seven minutes. You can pray the Angelus[39] at 6:00 a.m., noon, and 6:00 p.m., stopping what you are doing momentarily to ponder the Incarnation. If necessary, you can pray this silently in your heart, so as not to draw attention to

[39] You can find this prayer with the prayers and litanies later in this book.

yourself. This prayer has been prayed for centuries by other busy people who wanted to practice the discipline of stopping briefly throughout their day to pray. Every moment of the day is a grace from God. Let us remember to give that time back to Him out of love and obedience.

Holy Reminders as Gifts

> Friendship, of which God is the bond, is a valuable help in the work of expanding the glory of God. (St. Maximilian Kolbe)[40]

While hosting *EWTN Religious Catalogue*, I used every opportunity possible to stress the importance of giving holy reminders as gifts—for birthdays, weddings, anniversaries, Christmas, Easter, Baptisms, First Holy Communions, and other special occasions. But holy reminders are not limited to holidays and life's milestones. In fact, there is always a reason to give someone a holy reminder of our Faith and of the love of God.

Dave and I recently discovered the joy of giving holy reminders when visiting someone's house. It doesn't have to be anything terribly expensive, but the gesture matters. Whereas we used to default to bringing a bottle of wine or a dessert, we have started including any combination of votive candles, small pieces of sacred art, filled holy-water bottles, rosaries, devotional booklets, and novena Mass cards. These Mass cards are used to enroll a loved one in a novena of Masses; we give a small financial gift to a religious order, which then offers the Masses for the intentions of that loved one.

[40] *The Writings of St. Maximilian Maria Kolbe*, daily meditation from June 27, 1918.

Our family includes holy reminders in hospitality baskets for our own guests (alongside other creature comforts—bottled water, snacks, extra toiletries, a stack of towels, etc.). When a family friend stayed with us recently, he was overjoyed when we gifted him a Ven. Fr. Patrick Peyton rosary because he has a devotion to the late priest and firmly believes in the phrase made famous by Fr. Peyton: "The family that prays together stays together!" We didn't know that when we gave him the rosary, but God knew!

These holy reminders are special for a few reasons:

- They make a connection between fellow Catholics.
- They cultivate a spirit of Christian fellowship.
- They demonstrate thoughtfulness—especially if the holy reminder relates to a specific charism, cross, or occasion for someone—by allowing you to step outside your own life and consider the spiritual needs of others.
- They strengthen the Body of Christ through the fortification of Christian homes.

If a loved one has a devotion to St. Joseph, give him or her a St. Joseph votive candle, medal, or small statue. The Sleeping St. Joseph statue is an example of a unique gift that can be used in common living spaces, in bedrooms, or on an office desk.

If a family has recently moved to a new home and has not yet enthroned Jesus as King of their home and family, you could bring them a pair of prints of the Sacred Heart of Jesus and the Immaculate Heart of Mary. You also could bring a crucifix or a holy-water font.

If someone is battling cancer, a St. Peregrine holy reminder could be a good choice. If someone has recently suffered a death or another hardship, a booklet with a novena to Our Lady Undoer of Knots and a Blessed Mother votive candle would be nice.

If a visiting family has young kids, consider Catholic children's books or coloring books and a fresh box of crayons. I don't know about you, but I'm a sucker for a fresh box of crayons! These gifts also help redirect and settle the kids during get-togethers, which will allow the grown-ups to enjoy quality time together.

For a family with a new baby, a holy reminder of the child's patron saint or namesake would be a lifelong gift. You can also consider Catholic baby blankets, figurines of saints or biblical characters, sensory baby books, or baby-safe rosaries. I am a firm believer that the Blessed Mother doesn't mind baby-safe teething rosaries because they are one of the first ways children learn to find comfort in the Blessed Mother and the Rosary.

Even for non-Catholics, there are plenty of holy reminders to consider, such as a beautiful wall cross, a plaque with a Scripture passage, an image of Jesus, or a book about the Holy Land. I recently felt a strong calling to give a Miraculous Medal to our neighbor, who I knew was not Catholic. I can't explain the feeling, only that I knew I had to give it to him. Not only did he warmly receive the gift and promise to wear it, but he went on to show me the St. Florian medal he wears every day because, as a retired firefighter, he has a devotion to the saint. After the great suffering our beloved neighbor has endured throughout his life, I pray that he has been able to find peace and comfort under Our Lady's mantle.

If you are unsure of what to give someone, holy reminders related to classic Catholic devotions, such as the Divine Mercy, Our Lady of Mount Carmel, St. Michael the Archangel, and Our Lady of Guadalupe, are great choices. Pray that the Holy Spirit will guide you when selecting a gift.

Dave and I keep a stash of gifts in our home, like a mini *EWTN Religious Catalogue*, allowing us to choose something personal on the spur of the moment without having to pay for rush shipping or settle for less than what we would like to give. There's always an occasion to give a gift of encouragement, and if we listen to the interests and needs of our friends, we'll be able to discern a meaningful gift for them.

As recipients of holy reminders as gifts, Dave and I can testify to how special they are. We remember the people who gave us the various rosaries, crucifixes, statues, and sacred art we have in our home, and we pray for those people when we see those holy reminders. You can bestow the same joy through the act of giving holy reminders.

Let's be practical

Use the following chart to take inventory of the holy reminders mentioned here; consider which ones you already have in your home, in your car, and at your workplace, and so forth. Use the "Notes" column to designate the items you'd like to receive or give as gifts. This is a perfect way to plan ahead for birthdays, Baptisms, and other special occasions.

Pro tip

You don't have to invest in all of these holy reminders at once.

Holy Reminder	How many we have	How many we'd like	Notes
Divine Mercy images			
St. Benedict Medals			
Rosaries			
Brown Scapulars			
Miraculous Medals			
Saint medals			
Holy-water fonts			
Holy-water bottles			

Holy Reminder	How many we have	How many we'd like	Notes
Crucifixes			
Images and statues of Jesus			
Images and statues of the Blessed Mother			
Religious icons			
Religious wall art			
Holy reminders in the car			
Prayer cards			

Holy Reminder	How many we have	How many we'd like	Notes
Votive candles or blessed beeswax candles			
Saint jewelry			
Holy reminders for the kids or grandkids			
Devotional booklets			
Holy reminders for the outside or the garden			

"I hope you have a blessed reminder of the love of Jesus in your heart and in your home." (Mother Angelica)

11

Dedicated Family Prayer Time

I would wish that no day passed without your giving half-an-hour or an hour to the reading of some spiritual book.[41]

—St. Francis de Sales

Families nowadays are busy. We're constantly pulled in multiple directions: work, school, sports and other extracurricular activities, social life, errands, hobbies, housework, and so on. It's amazing how much is crammed into a single day!

It's easy to fall into making excuses for not spending time in prayer, especially together as a family: There's not enough time. We're too busy. Other things are more important.

The problem is not that there's not enough time. The problem is that there's not enough love.

To grow in our love of God, we need to spend time with Him. To grow in holiness as a family, we need to pray together. We're not

[41] *The Saint Francis de Sales Collection*, *Practical Piety*, pt. 4, chap. 34, "What a Person Engaged in the World Ought to Do in Order to Arrive at Perfection."

telling you which activities you and your family should be involved in. What we are saying is that parents who want to raise saints must make choices about how to spend the finite amount of time we get each day. How we choose to spend our time shows what and whom we value.

Here are some ways you can pray together as a family:

- In the morning, while everyone is getting ready for work and school, pray along with a recording of the Rosary, the Liturgy of the Hours, the Chaplet of the Divine Mercy, or another devotion.
- At the breakfast table or during your commute, ask each person to state his or her prayer intentions for the day. Depending on the length of your commute, you might be able to pray a couple of decades of the Rosary together.
- If you're at home with the kids in the morning, stream EWTN's daily Mass. My kids are the most docile in the morning, and this is a great time for us to enjoy a semi-quiet home.
- At 6:00 a.m., noon, and 6:00 p.m., or at one of those times, pray the Angelus together.
- At 3:00 p.m., pray the Chaplet of Divine Mercy. At the request of our kindergartener, we tend to use EWTN's On Demand platform to stream the Chaplet of Divine Mercy episode of the kids' show My Time with Jesus; on Fridays, we try to pray using the "Way of the Cross" episode of My Time with Jesus.
- After dinner, if you haven't done so already, pray the Rosary as part of a "family holy hour" (more on that later in this chapter).

No matter when and how you pray, be gentle and flexible. If you have young children, be attuned to when they are most likely to cooperate.

Sometimes the kids pay attention, and sometimes they play with toys. Dave and I try to maintain an atmosphere of peace (or an attempt at peace), always inviting our children to pray with us. The kids are usually pretty cuddly, so Dave and our eldest daughter will sit together and sometimes share a rosary, for example, while the younger two curl up on the couch with me.

This is not always a picture-perfect prayer time, and that's OK. Truly, what God cares about more than perfectly behaved children is our intentions as parents. We're desiring to have our entire family in the same room praying together. That's worth something, right? Of course it is!

Set your family up for success by creating an environment that is conducive to prayer and quiet time. This can include a prayer table or a family altar, with a crucifix, candles, exorcised incense, holy water, prayer cards, statues, and other sacramentals. If possible, remove distractions and dim the lights. Speak quietly and gently. Have a consistent prayer time so the children can be prepared. Encourage those who are able to kneel to do so. Do whatever you need to do to facilitate peace and quiet before entering into prayer.

There are plenty of ways to make praying together "kid friendly," such as by letting your kids have their own special rosaries in their favorite colors, by inviting them to share their prayer intentions, and by reading age-appropriate devotional books with them.

Obstacles to Praying Together as a Family

Here are four major obstacles to beginning to pray together as a family:

1. *Finding time*: Depending on your schedule, finding time to pray together might take some creativity or a reevaluation of priorities.

For the longest time, we tried to pray the Rosary in the evenings. For our family, that was a terrible idea! At least half the time, our kids were melting down. Dave made the brilliant suggestion that we begin praying the Rosary in the morning, after the kids eat breakfast, when they are most likely to be calm. To accomplish this, we had to reassess our situation and completely change the structure of our day, but praying the Rosary together is now 1,000 percent easier and more fruitful.

2. *Feeling uncomfortable*: If you've never prayed together as a family, let alone as a couple, this will probably feel unnatural and awkward. Thankfully, if your kids are young like ours, they won't remember what life was like before you started praying together regularly. If your kids are older, you can explain to them the change of heart you've had and how you now recognize the importance of praying together as a family. Who knows where sharing that vulnerability with them will take you! If you're not used to spontaneous prayer, of course it will feel forced at first. If praying the Rosary daily is not a habit yet, there might be some fumbling as you familiarize yourself with it.

In her apparitions at Fatima, Our Lady requested, "Pray the Rosary every day to bring peace to the world." Whether or not we feel like it, and whether or not we are comfortable with it, we should do it out of love for and obedience to God the Father and to the Blessed Mother. The more we pray the Rosary together, the more natural it will become, and the less the feelings of discomfort or awkwardness will be.

3. *Developing a habit*: There have been numerous studies on the time it takes to develop a habit. The numbers I hear vary but suggest at least sixty days. It is going to take a couple of months for you to get into

the habit of praying together regularly. And even then, if you're like the Cowdens, every day requires a deliberate choice to pray or not to pray. Don't give up! This is going to be one of the best changes you've ever made in your life—and definitely one that is going to bring your family closer as you grow in holiness together.

4. *Not knowing what to do*: The Catholic Church has more than two thousand years of saints, prayers, and devotions—an impossible amount of spiritual reading and exercises to do in a lifetime! Trying to practice many devotions and charisms is intimidating; by being faithful to a few devotions, you will find it much easier to be committed to prayer as you strive to grow in your love of God.

Surely God does not expect us to spend every hour of the day in silent prayer as a family. That would cause us to neglect our daily tasks! But if you could do, say, a "family holy hour" that includes any combination of the Rosary, the Chaplet of the Divine Mercy, the daily Mass readings, listening to the EWTN daily Mass homily, a litany corresponding with a season or an upcoming feast, spiritual reading, silent adoration, and singing one or two hymns, you would be offering a priceless gift to your family. God is never outdone as a giver! He will reward your effort and perseverance. That time spent away from the world and with the Lord will bring love, peace, joy, and strength to your family. It does not have to be exactly sixty minutes and likely will vary in length from season to season. The idea is to step away from the world intentionally and turn your eyes, ears, and hearts toward Heaven.

> Let not even one day pass without saying [the Rosary], no matter how burdened you may be with many cares and labors. (Pope Pius XI)[42]

[42] Encyclical *Ingravescentibus Malis* (September 29, 1937), no. 29.

Let's be practical

If we want to grow in our love of God and get our families to Heaven, we must step away from the world, rearrange our priorities, and actively seek ways to be with the Lord. By identifying the ideal prayer time, eliminating the distractions and hesitations, and creating a plan to overcome the roadblocks, we can make huge strides in our spiritual life and truly begin to raise saints.

Pro tip

As you begin to carve out time to pray together as a family, you will inevitably face hiccups and disruptions to the new routine. Be patient with one another and persevere together. God rewards our efforts!

How often are we praying together as a family?

How many days per week are we praying the Rosary as a family?

What is our ideal prayer time? What is the best location (room)? Which things are most conducive to prayer (e.g., incense and candles)? Which devotions, spiritual reading, and sacred hymns are best for our family?

What roadblocks prevent us from praying together daily?

What steps can we take to overcome those roadblocks?

Do we have a prayer table? Which holy reminders do we have or want to have on our prayer table?

What time of day will we commit to praying together as a family?

"I would encourage you to thank God for the faith you have, and ask Him to increase it." (Mother Angelica)

12

Daily Mass

Know, O Christian, that the Mass is the holiest act of religion. You cannot do anything to glorify God more, nor profit your soul more, than by devoutly assisting at it, and assisting as often as possible.[43]

—St. Peter Julian Eymard

At the beginning of 2020, our son had just turned one. God bless this little boy, who was doing his best during Mass. We'd go to 8:00 a.m. Mass, when he was at his most docile, and we'd load him up with a bottle of milk so he'd be quiet and content. We sat toward the front of the church, and Dave usually had to stand in the back of the church with him for only the last ten to fifteen minutes of Mass.

Our eldest was three, and she would sit quietly in the pew, sometimes coloring, sometimes flipping through her toddlers' missal.

[43] St. Peter Julian Eymard, *The Holy Sacrifice*, trans. E. Lummis, no. 1, quoted in *Sentinel* (July 1901), https://archive.org/stream/sentinelofblesse00newyuoft/sentinelofblesse00newyuoft_djvu.txt.

We had a great system and felt as though we were finally able to start paying better attention during Mass.

Then a global pandemic broke out. Churches closed, the world shut down, and we were unable to take our kids to Mass. We waited months to return, and the mandatory lockdowns lasted long enough to undo the good work we had done in training our kids. We suddenly dreaded taking them to Mass because neither behaved as well as we'd like, and the thought crossed our minds to start going to Mass separately while the other stayed home with the kids.

But then Dave had an idea: "Why don't we start taking them to daily Mass?"

My thoughts were, "Are you kidding me? We can't even get them to sit still at Mass *once* a week! What makes you think I'd want to subject myself to that *repeatedly*?"

But Dave was onto something.

Our kids couldn't sit still because they weren't used to being in the pews anymore. They weren't used to having to sit quietly for an hour at a time. They weren't used to going without the stimulation they have with their toys at home.

We made the decision to take them to daily Mass more regularly. Wouldn't you know, as soon as we started taking them regularly, they started to behave better. They got used to the routine. They got used to getting dressed and piling into the car. They got used to the cadence of the Mass, and they learned what to do and what to say. They got used to the quiet.

Sometimes Dave takes our son to the early morning Mass. Sometimes he takes our two oldest kids to noon Mass. And we all enjoy going together to the evening Mass. Our eldest likes going to daily Mass with "just Mom," and we enjoy the special time together.

When we started going to daily Mass, I admit that there were times when I felt, "Wow, this is eating up a lot of our time." *How little love I had in my heart!* The remedy for this, as you might have guessed, is going to Mass. I needed it!

In terms of fitting Mass into our schedule, we realized we had no excuses for not attending daily Mass a couple of times per week.

A tired parent like me might think there's no time for daily Mass during the week. The reality is, however, that if we want to grow in our love of God, we need to spend more time with Him. And isn't Mass the best way to spend our time anyway?

Once Dave and I came to this realization, the choice was obvious: we were going to do whatever it took to make time for daily Mass. Thankfully, in our town, there are at least twenty Catholic churches within a twenty-minute drive of our home. We even have a Catholic church two blocks from our home!

If you currently have issues or hesitation about committing to daily Mass every week, start with the First Friday and First Saturday devotions. Our Lord and Our Lady offer tremendous graces to those who are faithful to these devotions.

First Friday Devotion

For nine consecutive months, do the following on the First Friday of each month:

1. Attend Holy Mass.
2. Receive the Eucharist.
3. Go to Confession within eight days.
4. Do these things with the intention of honoring the Sacred Heart of Jesus and making reparation for blasphemies against Him.

First Saturday Devotion

For five consecutive months, do the following on the First Saturday of each month:

1. Go to Confession within eight days.
2. Receive Holy Communion.
3. Pray the Rosary.
4. Keep Mary company while meditating on the mysteries of the Rosary for fifteen minutes, specifically with the intention of making reparation for blasphemies against the Immaculate Heart of Mary.

Every decision we make to choose God over the world will bear good fruit. Every effort we make to love and serve God will be met with His love and mercy.

I don't think it's a stretch to claim that daily Mass has changed our lives completely. After all, receiving Jesus in the Eucharist *should* be life-changing! It's clear to Dave and me that we've benefited from the graces of the sacraments, from the quiet time in prayer, and from planning our day around the Lord.

If you've not made it to daily Mass lately, or ever, we invite you to change your life for the better and to be receptive to the many graces awaiting you! God loves you so much. As you grow in love of Him, you will begin to see how greatly He loves you and how many blessings He wishes to bestow on parents who bring their children to see Him.

Let's be practical

Which parishes near you have daily Mass, and at what times? At what times do they have Confession?

Pro tip

Make a schedule with your spouse to plan the day around Mass, and not the other way around!

Parish	Day	Time	Confession times

Enter the date for each First Friday you honor:

Enter the date for each First Saturday you honor:

"Strengthen my love and my gratitude for this tremendous gift. Give me the faith to understand that the Eucharist makes everything possible." (Mother Angelica)

13

Family Litany of Saints

Now, we must help each other get to heaven.[44]

—Bl. Charles of Austria

In our efforts to grow in the love of God and get our families to Heaven, we should strive to imitate the saints, who proved that it *is* possible to grow in the love of God and get to Heaven, even in the modern day.

The Church has recognized thousands of saints by name, specifically identifying them as being worthy of imitation. We ought to study their spiritual lives, look to them for guidance, and ask for their prayers.

We can encourage our children to befriend the saints as well. Dave and I explain to our children, in an age-appropriate way, that the saints are real people who live in Heaven with Jesus. They love God very much, and they want *us* to love Him more too! As we pray for our friends when they need help, the saints pray for us.

[44] Quoted in Denis Kitzinger, "Blessed Karl von Habsburg," *Crisis Magazine*, March 27, 2102, https://www.crisismagazine.com/2012/blessed-karl-von-habsburg.

You can ask them for anything you need, and they will be happy to help. They show us how to be holy, how to love God, and how to love others.

In the final section of this book, we present a variety of saints whom parents can befriend. Once we get to know these saints, we can help our children get to know them too. We can give our children holy reminders of these saints; we can talk to the saints regularly because they are always with us; and we can cultivate an appreciation of their heroic virtue.

We see this in our daughter Gianna, who loves her namesake and desires to be a doctor just like St. Gianna. Gigi has a doctor's kit with stethoscope and a white lab coat, and she likes to give her siblings, her parents, and her stuffed animals thorough "checkups."

In our own lives, we have seen that while we've chosen certain saints to befriend, there are others who have chosen us—such as St. Thérèse, St. John Bosco, St. Joan of Arc, St. Jane Frances de Chantal, St. Polycarp, and Servant of God Rhoda Wise. We pray that more saints will make themselves known to us and to our children and that they will gently lead us on the way to holiness.

A unique way to ask for the intercession of your favorite saints is with a family litany of saints. We developed ours organically over the years, adding saints and holy people who are namesakes of our children and godchildren. Your litany can be as long or as short as you'd like. The general idea is that it should include the saints your family calls upon every day for guidance.

Our litany, which we pray at the end of every Rosary, includes the following:

Holy Mary, Mother of God, pray for us.
St. Joseph ...
St. Gianna Molla ...
St. Thérèse of Lisieux ...
St. Anthony of Padua ...
St. Francis of Assisi ...
St. Clare of Assisi ...
St. Rita of Cascia ...
Sts. Louis and Zélie Martin ...
St. Thomas Aquinas ...
Servant of God Rhoda Wise ...
Our holy guardian angels ...
All holy men and women of God ...

We add other saints on their feast days or for particular intentions, but the list above is the core group we go to every single day in prayer. Dave and I have been praying specifically for the intercession of St. Joseph and St. Gianna (our Confirmation saints) since we started dating, and I love seeing how the list has grown to include our children's patron saints, godchildren's patron saints, and saints for particular intentions.

Our five-year-old is quite enthusiastic about the litany of saints. She likes to yell, "Pray for us!" And she knows why we pray for the intercession of each of the saints. We've found this to be greatly beneficial in introducing our children to the intercession of the saints and calling on those saints regularly for help as we grow in holiness.

Let's be practical

At the end of this book, we provide space for your family to create your own litany of saints. Hang it near your prayer table or in a common space where you can be reminded to invoke their intercession often. *All ye holy men and women of God, pray for us!*

Pro tip

If there are some saints your kids are familiar with already, invite your kids to name a few they would like to include in your litany.

"Saints aren't just ancient figures with polished halos. And anyways, those saints were just as imperfect as you are. They had the same problems and temptations and weaknesses you have." (Mother Angelica)

14

Individual Prayer

In order then that we also may extinguish all the furnace of disordered pleasure here, and so escape the hell that is there, let these each day be our counsels, our cares, and our practice, drawing towards us the favor of God, both by our full purpose concerning good works, and by our frequent prayers. For thus even those things which appear insupportable now, will be most easy and light, and lovely.[45]

—St. John Chrysostom

There was a time in our marriage when Dave and I didn't leave the house to go on dates. We made all sorts of excuses for not going out—young children, new baby on the way, lack of a reliable babysitter, not wanting to burden family members to watch the kids, global pandemic, trying to save money, and so on.

[45] St. John Chrysostom, Homily 16 on Matthew, trans. George Prevost, rev. M. B. Riddle, in *Nicene and Post-Nicene Fathers*, First Series, vol. 10, ed. Philip Schaff (Buffalo, NY: Christian Literature Publishing, 1888), revised and edited for New Advent by Kevin Knight, http://www.newadvent.org/fathers/200116.htm.

If you're a tired parent, you know how easily your relationship can take a back burner to the children and keeping up with the house. Sometimes it seems completely unfeasible for you and your spouse to step away from the home to take time for each other. There's so much effort exerted throughout the day and into the evening that, by the time the kids go to bed, there usually is no time or energy for much else.

For Dave and me, however, the lack of special date time reserved for each other took its toll. We realized that, despite the time we spent together with the kids underfoot, we still needed designated time to focus on each other. We needed to have adult conversations, listen to each other, "date" each other, and remind each other of how much we love each other.

Yes, we're married "till death do us part," but that doesn't mean we have to stop trying! The same goes for our relationship with God.

A huge part of what we advocate for in the lives of tired parents is making prayer flow freely throughout the day. Every breath can be a prayer, and every household task can be offered to God, thus becoming a prayer. Every moment can be an opportunity to bask in God's love and desire closeness with Him.

But if we really want to grow in our love of God, we need to make time to be alone face-to-face with Him. We need to carve out part of every single day to be with Him—praying, listening, and adoring Him. We see in the Gospels that even Jesus took time away to pray alone. He did this up to forty days at a time! We are not called to pray in seclusion for forty days, but we should be making time to pray every day.

Dave and I are no strangers to excuses for not praying—the lack of time, the lack of energy, the kids' schedules, the work schedules, the demanding house projects, and so on.

There's not enough time to commit to prayer, but how much time is there for TV, social media, and mindlessly surfing the Internet?

The reality is that we have to make the time because our relationship with God matters. Whether we utilize a block of time in the morning before the kids get up or wait until the kids are asleep, we need to take a hard look at our daily routines to see when we will show God that He matters in our lives. We have to show our desire to give Him dedicated, uninterrupted (or mostly uninterrupted) time and attention.

The early hours of the morning are best suited for Dave. For me, the late evening works best.

When Dave and I prioritize spending time together outside the home, or at least inside the home with a designated "date" time, it strengthens our marriage. We are more connected to each other. We are rejuvenated. We anticipate the next time we can spend together. And we're better able to meet the needs of our children.

How much more do our lives improve when we make time for God?

Here some are ways you can prioritize dedicated, individual prayer time in your daily life:

- Set aside nonnegotiable, undisturbed prayer time. If necessary, inform your kids so they will understand: "Dad is going to spend twenty minutes in prayer. It's important for him to talk to and listen to God."

- Moms, don't be afraid to leave the home for a short time. Your husband will be happy to tend to the kids while you spend time with Jesus. Find a nearby church (it's a bonus if there's Eucharistic Adoration!) or a quiet outdoor space to pray in.

- If you commute to work, budget a few extra minutes when you arrive at work or before you leave to sit in your car and pray the Liturgy of the Hours or the Chaplet of Divine Mercy or to read the daily Mass readings or spend a few minutes on spiritual reading.

- When you and your spouse plan your designated date times inside or outside the home, begin and end with a brief period of silent prayer, thanking God for your spouse, praying for his or her intentions, and praising God for His goodness.

Let's get practical

Examine your current prayer routine and consider the ways you can do more to grow in your love of God. He desires to spend time with you and show you His love. How will you make more time for Him?

Pro tip

Amid the busyness of life, prayer can go by the wayside. Remind yourself that this time alone with Him is nonnegotiable, a joyful duty.

How much time am I committing daily to personal prayer with God?

What does my current personal prayer time look like now—prayers, spiritual reading, sacred music, location?

What does my ideal prayer time look like?

What are the roadblocks that prevent me from making the most of my time alone with God?

What steps will I take to remove distractions and excuses?

"Constant prayer is the deep assurance within my heart that God is in charge, and I have no need to worry. That's what it means to pray continually, because prayer is union with God." (Mother Angelica)

15

Spontaneous Prayer and Offering Joys and Sufferings

If, after having, during life, welcomed to your embrace all things that have come from God, you in like manner embrace death also in order to accomplish his divine will, you will certainly secure your salvation and die the death of a saint.[46]

—St. Alphonsus Liguori

Earlier in the book, we mentioned how our prayer life changed drastically when we had children. One of the ways it changed for the better was our adoption of spontaneous prayer and learning to offer to God our joys and sufferings throughout the day.

Sometimes it's hard for parents to get those big chunks of quiet prayer time. During the day, there are distractions, annoyances, conflicts, and plenty of opportunities to complain. But when we

[46] St. Alphonsus Liguori, *The Way of Salvation and of Perfection* (London: Catholic Way Publishing, 2016), pt. 3, sect. 3, chap. 4, "God Wishes Only Our Good."

turn every moment into an opportunity for prayer, we change the purpose, and sometimes the outcome, of our days.

Dave and I refer to the spontaneous prayers prayed throughout the day as "passing prayers." You'll see those in the back of the book with the saints' reflections and prayers. These passing prayers are quick, memorized prayers or off-the-cuff prayers that allow us to be in constant conversation with God, the Blessed Mother, and the saints.

A well-known passing prayer is called the Jesus Prayer: "Jesus Christ, Son of God, have mercy on me, a sinner." Another is "Jesus, Mary, and Joseph, I love you; save souls."

Here are a few other off-the-cuff prayers you can pray:

Jesus, I need help being patient.

Mama Mary, what would you do?

St. Joseph, be with me as I work today.

Guardian angels, help us pray this Rosary.

Not only can we pray these short, heartfelt prayers throughout the day, but we can also offer God our joys and sufferings, the good and the not-so-good that happens throughout the day.

Growing up, I heard a lot of "Offer it up!" I didn't fully understand what that meant or how my suffering could be used for the good of other souls. I didn't realize that "offering it up" was a means by which I could participate in Jesus' suffering on the Cross. I didn't understand that by using my sorrows and trials as a means of prayer, I was, in fact, partaking in redemptive suffering—a more perfect kind of love—just like Jesus.

Since we are all members of the Body of Christ, every prayer we offer up strengthens the Body and saves souls. Since suffering exists because of man's fallen nature, we participate in the overcoming of sin and death. That's quite a compelling reason to offer every moment to God, for love of Him and love of our neighbor! Here are several examples of things you can offer to God:

- If you wake up to the sun peeking in your window and it looks as if it will be a beautiful day, offer a prayer of thanksgiving for God's goodness.
- If you wake up to a thunderstorm when your family planned a picnic at the park, offer your disappointment for a soul in Purgatory.
- If your day is going smoothly and you're enjoying quality time with your family, offer your joy in thanksgiving for the gift of your spouse and your children.
- If you're feeling overwhelmed with balancing work and home responsibilities, offer your worries for the soul of a deceased family member.
- If one of your children wakes you in the middle of the night because dinner upset his stomach, offer your tiredness for those without food and for the homeless.
- If your child reaches a new milestone with school, a musical instrument, or a sport, offer your joy in thanksgiving for his or her health.
- If your child repeatedly tests your patience, offer your frustrations for the salvation of your child.
- If you enjoy a loving and relaxing date night with your spouse, offer that joy for the future vocations of your children.

I could go on and on. Most likely, you are keenly aware of the joys and sorrows you regularly face. Think of how you can offer those for the good of souls and for your family's holiness.

Whatever roadblocks or trials you're facing, you can make good come from the suffering. You can pray, "Jesus, I'm placing this burden at the foot of Your Cross, and I ask for the grace to bear my suffering with love."

1 Thessalonians 5:16–18 says, "Rejoice always, pray constantly, give thanks in all circumstances; for this is the will of God in Christ Jesus for you."

Let's be practical

What brings you joy? What causes you sorrow? Every moment of the day and every encounter offers an opportunity to offer joys and sufferings to God. Be specific about how you want to use these to glorify God and to pray for souls who need it most.

Pro tip

It's never too early to show your children the value of offering joys and sufferings to God. Help your children make their own lists of things to offer to God, daily or weekly. Read and pray them aloud together.

Lord, I offer this *joy* ...	in thanksgiving for:

Lord, I offer this *suffering* ...	for this soul or cause:

"Thank You, Jesus, for the graces and gifts of this day. I praise You for the sorrow that detached me and the joy that made me so aware of Your Presence. I love You, Lord God—make me like You." (Mother Angelica)

16

Prayer-Intention Calendar

O Christ, sweet Jesus, give me this holy charity, that I may persevere in doing good and never give it up; for he who possesses charity is founded in You, the living rock, and by following Your example, he learns from You how to love his Creator and his neighbor.[47]

— St. Catherine of Siena

For the month of November, Dave and I create a calendar of prayer intentions, and we offer our joys and sufferings of each day for a particular departed soul (November is dedicated to the Poor Souls and to praying in a special way for their release from Purgatory). Trust me when I say that daily burdens are much easier to bear when they are offered for the salvation of a departed soul!

In years past, our prayer calendar has included names of family members, friends, former co-workers, relatives of acquaintances, people we learned of from the news or social media, unnamed wayward souls near death, and souls who were just about ready to enter Heaven. We'd fill in their names on one

[47] Quoted in *Divine Intimacy*, no. 273, "The Good Samaritan."

of our wall calendars, and then we'd offer our day—including Mass, the Rosary, and all the day's trials—for the person assigned to that day.

This is a great way for your family to do a spiritual work of mercy (praying for the living and the dead), but it doesn't have to be unique to November. In fact, you can and should offer every day of the year for souls and other intentions! Surely you can think of people who need prayers. When someone mentions a joy, such as the news of a baby on the way, or a sorrow, such as an illness or a death, you can offer to have your entire family pray for that person.

You don't need to get fancy or complicated with the calendar. You can use a simple wall calendar or print one from the Internet. You can even use a calendar app, although it's better to have one the entire family can see at any time.

Simply write a person's name and an intention in each box. You can fill these in ahead of time or decide on the day's intention in the morning. It was helpful for us to map out our intentions for departed souls in advance and then to fill in boxes as needed. Fill in names as soon as you hear of an intention. (I don't know about you, but if I don't write it down immediately, I am liable to forget!) You can remember family members and friends on their birthdays or anniversaries or remember souls on the days of their death. Or you can write "a poor soul who has no one to pray for him" or "the conversion of a soul in danger of Hell."

You could also fill in nine days at a time for novenas to Our Lady Undoer of Knots, the Divine Mercy, and so forth.

Making a calendar is an excellent way to unite the family in praying for a particular intention, and a surefire way to remember whom you are praying for throughout the day.

Let's be practical

Start a prayer intention calendar using a wall calendar, a calendar template, or simply a list of dates.

Pro tip

Don't forget to pray for deceased family members, priests and religious, and those who have no one else to pray for them!

Sample Calendar

Sunday	In thanksgiving for our family and for all God's blessings	Grandpa Charles and Grandma Gloria (RIP)
Monday	For a productive work week for Mom	An unknown soul in Purgatory (RIP)
Tuesday	For the help of our guardian angels	Uncle Bob (RIP)
Wednesday	For someone who is going to die today (St. Joseph, pray for that person!)	Nicholas B. (RIP)
Thursday	In reparation for blasphemies against the Holy Eucharist	Aunt Mary (RIP)

Friday	For more perfect Christian love	Grandma Fran and Great Grandma (RIP)
Saturday	For greater love of Jesus through Mary	Grandma Connie (RIP)

"Sometimes my worst day—one filled with pain and suffering—in the eyes of God is my best day if I've born it cheerfully and I've born it with love." (Mother Angelica)

17

Being Catholic 24/7

You cannot be half a saint;
you are either a full one or none at all.[48]

—St. Thérèse of Lisieux

With our Faith, it's all or nothing. Either we are faithful Catholics, or we are not Catholics at all. We must be deliberate in choosing holiness every day. It sounds harsh, but that is the reality. If something is not leading us toward Heaven, it is leading us away from Heaven.

We must root out the things that lead us away from God. We must specifically identify and remove them from our lives. It requires making difficult decisions, but they will lead to our good, our holiness, and our eternal reward.

[48] Letter 252, to Fr. Maurice Belliere, quoted in a conference by Antonio Maria Sicari, O.C.D., "Saint Teresa of the Child Jesus and the Priesthood," Vatican website, https://www.vatican.va/roman_curia/congregations/cclergy/documents/jub_preti_20000517_sicari_en.html.

We not only must root out the bad, but we must also add in the good. Dave and I have been doing more spiritual reading and reading Faith-based books to our kids more often.

To be honest, when we have the truth, beauty, and goodness of the Catholic Faith and a flourishing spiritual life and are making strides in helping our children grow in holiness, we are naturally less attracted to the things of the world. Detachment from the attractions of the world allows us to give ourselves more freely to God, as opposed to being slaves to the empty pleasures of the world.

Being Catholic 24/7 means striving to live every moment for God's glory, to make every breath a prayer, and to give every ounce of energy to loving and serving God in this life so we can enjoy eternal happiness with Him in the next. We can view it as a constant struggle, which it is in its own right, or we can view it as a joyful opportunity to be fully alive and fully in communion with God. Doesn't that sound wonderful?

Let's be practical

What is preventing you from being Catholic 24/7?

Pro tip

This is not a one-and-done process. It involves daily conversion and daily decisions to act in accordance with God's will. Take it one day at a time as you learn to identify ways you can detach yourself from the world and grow closer to God.

What is preventing us from being Catholic 24/7?

What would our family life be like if we were Catholic 24/7?

Of the ten foundation blocks of prayer in this book (house blessing and enthronement of the Most Sacred Heart of Jesus; consecration to the Blessed Mother and St. Joseph; holy reminders; dedicated family prayer time; daily Mass; family litany of saints; individual prayer; spontaneous prayer and offering joys and sufferings; prayer-intention calendar; being Catholic 24/7), which will we try to improve upon most?

"Don't imagine you can be a saint lickety-split. You have to go through the process, and that could take a lifetime." (Mother Angelica)

18

Examination of Conscience for Parents

The charity which burned in the household at Nazareth should be an inspiration for every family. All the Christian virtues should flourish in the family, unity should thrive, and the example of its virtuous living should shine brightly.[49]

—Pope St. John XXIII

Sainthood is the goal for our family, and along the way, we will inevitably slip up. Thank God for the gifts of forgiveness and absolution!

An examination of conscience is a wonderful tool for preparing for the sacrament of Confession. It can also be used on a daily or weekly basis to examine our faults and failings and try to do better. The intent is not to be overly scrupulous or disheartened, but we've seen in our own lives that there are certain habitual sins that affect our family directly.

[49] Pope St. John XXIII, encyclical *Ad Petri cathedram* (June 29, 1959), no. 57.

We compiled this examination of conscience for parents based on the Ten Commandments. It is meant not to cover all the potential sins parents could commit but to offer a starting point for rooting out vices and growing in virtue for the sake of sanctifying the family.

1. I am the Lord thy God. Thou shalt not have strange gods before me.

- Do I show my children that I put God first in my life?
- Have I given the impression that other things are more important than prayer, Mass, and the teachings of the Church?
- Do I try to make good use of my time, so we have time for individual and family prayer?
- Have I modeled for my children an unhealthy attachment to sports, media consumption, recreation, or other worldly activities?

2. Thou shalt not take the Name of the Lord thy God in vain.

- Have I used God's Name in vain?
- Do I model clean language for my children? Do I avoid swearing and vulgarity?
- Have I listened to vulgar or impure music or watched impure movies or TV shows?
- Do I use suggestive language or humor? Do my children hear me tell dirty jokes?

3. Keep the Sabbath holy.

- What have we done to set aside Sunday as the Lord's Day, making God the center of our family's day?
- Do I attempt to plan ahead so that on Sunday mornings, we can have minimal chaos, get to Mass early, and have time to pray before Mass begins?
- Have we arranged our schedule so as to avoid doing unnecessary labor on Sunday?
- Have we arranged our schedule so as to avoid making others do unnecessary labor on Sunday?

4. Honor thy father and thy mother.

- In what ways do we show our children that we honor our parents?
- Have we spoken kindly about our parents, especially in front of our children?
- Are we impatient with our parents, especially in how they interact with our children?
- Have we been willing to assist our parents with their needs, particularly as they grow older?

5. Thou shalt not kill.

- Do we focus on promoting a culture of life in our home, respecting life from the moment of conception to natural death?
- Do our children see us promoting change in a peaceful way, never suggesting or excusing violence?

- Are violent video games and movies allowed in our home? What about music with aggressive lyrics?
- Have we intentionally done things to abuse our bodies, such as drinking in excess, smoking, using illicit drugs, performing unsafe recreational activities, binging on foods? Have we set a bad example with these behaviors?

6. Thou shalt not commit adultery.

- Have we kept our home free from pornography, nudity, promiscuity, and illicit media?
- Do we model modesty in clothing and behavior for our children?
- What have we done to encourage modesty, chastity, and purity in our children (in age-appropriate ways)?
- Are we using any form of contraception, even though it is forbidden?

7. Thou shalt not steal.

- Are we modeling honesty for our children when it comes to financial transactions?
- Have our children seen us take what isn't ours or lie to save or make money?
- Have we ever lied on our taxes or to our insurance companies or committed any type of fraud?
- Do I "borrow" things from friends or family with no intention of returning them?

8. Thou shalt not bear false witness against thy neighbor.

- Do I lie in front of my kids, even if they're "small" lies?
- Am I modeling integrity, or do I present different versions of myself in front of my children, depending on who is around?
- Have I lied to or intentionally withheld information from my spouse?
- Do I gossip, slander, or detract?

9 and 10. Thou shalt not covet thy neighbor's wife or goods.

- Do my spouse and I foster an attitude of contentment, or are we constantly trying to "keep up with the Joneses"?
- Have I acted selfishly or greedily in front of my children?
- Do our children see us prioritizing material goods or superficial relationships?
- Have we ever made decisions about appearances or relationships based on what others would think of us?
- Do I wish my spouse were more like someone else—a friend, a celebrity, or a social media influencer?
- Do I resent friends or others for their relationships, wishing I had the same?

"If you examine yourself honestly, you'll be able to say, 'Well, I'm unkind. Well, I'm uncharitable. I'm caustic. I'm critical. I'm jealous. I'm without compassion.' All of these things you can't get to Heaven with. It's very simple to know and to judge yourself before you die." (Mother Angelica)

PART 3

Stepping Forward in Faith

19

Work Smarter, Not Harder

Never give up prayer. And should you find dryness and difficulty, persevere in it for this very reason. God often desires to see what love your soul has, and love is not tried by ease and satisfaction.[50]

—St. John of the Cross

Parenting is difficult. You know that. Even parents with the best intentions will fail at times.

Parents who are faithful to prayer, who diligently raise their children in the Faith, and who are open to life will face challenges. Even parents who frequent the sacraments, who attend daily Mass, and who imitate the lives of the saints will be tested.

The one constant in life is God's love for us. By trusting in His divine plan, we will have the sure hope that good can come from all our trials. Our responsibility is to persevere with obedience, faithfulness, and love. It is also our responsibility to do whatever

[50] *Degrees of Perfection*, no. 9, in *The Collected Works of John of the Cross*, trans. Kieran Kavanaugh and Otilio Rodriguez (Washington, DC: ICS Publications, 1991), 729.

we can to make our homes and lives conducive to receiving God's grace.

Now that we've established the foundations of prayer, we can reflect on how to further improve our lives, grow in our love of God, and get our families to Heaven.

We don't mind calling ourselves tired parents, but let's be clear. We are not advocating needlessly subjecting ourselves to exhaustion, to the point where we cannot serve our families. Not only that, but the more time and energy we waste on things that could be done more efficiently, the less time we have for prayer and bonding with our spouses and kids.

There are important corporal needs parents must meet to take care of the family. Here are a few recommendations:

- Eat during the day. Eat breakfast. Coffee is not breakfast. The crust you cut off your kid's sandwich is not lunch. Do not neglect to refuel your body. You cannot serve your family if you do not feed your body. Even during times when fasting and abstinence are required, they should never be practiced at the expense of meeting your family's needs. (For example, pregnant and nursing mothers are exempt from fasting because the child depends on receiving nutrition from the mother's body.)

- Practice good sleep hygiene. Put away your phone before you climb into bed. Have a consistent bedtime routine with a consistent bedtime. If you need naps during the day, make them part of your schedule. If you're helping your children through sleep regressions, be patient with them and with yourself, and seek help from a trusted professional.

- Exercise. It doesn't have to be strenuous. It doesn't have to be outside the home. It doesn't have to involve heavy equipment or expensive memberships. Play outside with your kids, use some dance workout videos, or go on walks with your family. The fresh air, increased heart rate, and change of scenery will perk you up and offer additional health benefits to decrease lethargy.

- Consider cutting back on extra responsibilities. I'm not going to tell you what's too much, but I'm confident you'll be able to prioritize better when you start praying and re-orienting your family toward God.
- Be attentive to your health. There are some situations where you might have a legitimate health issue that is causing chronic fatigue—an autoimmune disorder, an undiagnosed food allergy, hormone imbalances, or other undiagnosed diseases. If you suspect that something like this is the case, please see your doctor or trusted health-care professional.

There are also household routines and lifestyle choices you can adopt to make your prayer life easier to sustain:

- Serve meals at the same time every day. This consistency offers predictability for every member of the family and reduces the instances of hunger-related meltdowns. Make a meal plan and shop for groceries accordingly.
- Write out a rough schedule for the day. Our day goes so much more smoothly when everyone is on the same page about the plan. Even if something unexpected puts the day a bit behind schedule, the written game plan can reorient the family and prevent the day from being completely derailed.
- As much as possible, reduce or eliminate screen time during prayer. If you are tempted to overuse your phone or TV, your

prayer time should be a respite from the media. Catholic apps can be very useful, but if they feed a phone addiction, you're better off praying without them. For two thousand years, Catholics didn't need apps to become saints! Putting away your phone can be a small act of mortification that does wonders for your mind and soul.

- Change the choice of music you listen to during the day. Instead of mainstream genres, opt for music that will lift your mind and heart to God (classical, Christian, hymns, etc.). We've found that playing quiet classical music or sacred hymns positively impacts everyone's moods and offers a chance to quiet our hearts and offer silent prayers to God.

- Keep your holy reminders and spiritual reading organized and in places where you can find them easily. Items used for family prayer time should be kept together; prayer books and devotional booklets should be in designated places (on the nightstand, in your office desk, in your purse or diaper bag, etc.). It seems as though these items grow little legs and wander off, but keeping them organized will make it much easier to be consistent in prayer.

- Surround yourself with other Catholics who are trying to live the Faith. They don't necessarily need to have children the same age as yours, but having fellow parents to lean on and pray with fortifies everyone involved.

We ought to do whatever we can to make our lives a little bit easier. When the house is under control, we are more at peace and our minds are freed to give glory to God.

20

Mother Angelica's Wisdom for Tired Parents

The essence of holiness is not doing great things,
but in doing ordinary things with great love
for God and neighbor.

—Mother Angelica

Mother Angelica has been a spiritual mother to Dave and me for a long time, even more so when I began working for EWTN. She had the gift of being able to say exactly what I needed to hear. It was as if the message she was delivering in her books and TV shows was for me alone.

When we got the call on Easter Sunday in 2016 telling us that Mother had passed away, we knew that everything was going to change, though it's hard to explain in writing. Since EWTN's launch in 1981, Mother Angelica had always been praying fervently for the network and acting with complete trust in Divine Providence. When she died, I didn't fully understand how powerful her intercession would be or how her example of trusting could be translated to my personal role in the mission of EWTN.

Dave and I attended Mother Angelica's visitation on March 30, 2016, at the Shrine of the Most Blessed Sacrament in Hanceville, Alabama. When we approached her in her casket, I remember gazing upon her body and asking her, "Mother, is this it? This can't be it."

In my heart, I felt as if she were chuckling and telling me, "Oh, sweetheart, we're just getting started. Now get cracking!"

I was about six months pregnant with our first child, and I had no idea what Mother meant. All I knew was that I was very pregnant, very overwhelmed, and very unsure of what was happening next for EWTN and for my own life. I thought it was impossible for me to continue being a TV producer while caring for a newborn baby. Dave was in the first months of his competitive doctoral program and was not permitted to work due to the intense workload. Daycare was not an option. We had been married less than a year and were still adjusting to newlywed life while living in a tiny, one-bedroom apartment. There was a lot going on!

Yet somehow, it was as though Mother knew just what to say to simultaneously comfort me and embolden me to keep moving forward in faith, which she called "one foot on the ground, one foot in the air, and a queasy feeling in the stomach."

Amid immense stress and uncertainty, Mother Angelica taught us to trust God completely. Not only did everything work out, but it worked out better than we expected! I was able to continue working for EWTN, we could meet our family's needs, and the other issues worked themselves out.

Parenting requires a lot of faith—having it, practicing it, keeping it, and sharing it. Mother knew how to do all of these; she modeled them time and time again, and she's a perfect example to imitate. As they say, "Mother knows best!"

Her way of holiness is simple yet profound. She abandoned herself to God's will, trusted in Divine Providence, and wasn't afraid to do crazy things to accomplish her God-given mission.

Here are ten tips for parents, based on Mother Angelica's timeless wisdom:

1. When you're struggling to be patient, Mother says:

> When I was a young novice, I used to pray in the early morning, "Dear Lord, today I am going to be patient come hell or high water." And by nine o'clock came hell and high water! I blew it!... Patience is adjusting your time to God's timing.

2. When you're feeling dryness in prayer, Mother says:

> I guarantee that if your soul is at peace because God is in charge, you'll pray without ceasing, though you may not say prayers and you may not think beautiful meditations.

3. When you're feeling anxious about what the future holds, Mother says:

> We worry about the past, we worry about the future, and we worry about the present. I mean, what worry-warts we are! We worry instead of saying, "He's watching me. He sees me and He loves me." That's why He says, "Courage. It is I. Do not be afraid."

4. When you're trying to defeat sinful anger, Mother says:

> St. Jerome had a terrible temper. He would hit himself with a rock every time he lost his temper. I'd be dead as

> a doornail, with no ribs, if I did that.... Don't say, "If it weren't for that person, I could be holy." No, you can be holy *because of* that person.

5. When you're asking why God allows suffering in your life, Mother says:

> Next to my vocation, the greatest gift I have is the pain I carry every day, because it forces me to cling to Jesus.... Holiness is not for wimps and the Cross is not negotiable, sweetheart, it's a requirement.

6. When you get pushback from others for the Faith you're living, Mother says:

> It's your obligation to speak the truth, and everyone can either take it or leave it. But truth must be in us. We live in such a poverty of truth today.... God wants you to be in the world, but so different from the world that you will change it. Get cracking!

7. When it's difficult to love your neighbor, Mother says:

> If I prefer the good of my neighbor to myself, I can rest assured that I love my neighbor in the same way God loves me, because that's how He loves me in the Eucharist. If I can be dependent, self-sacrificing, humble, loving, and compassionate, then I love as God loves; I love as God loves me.

8. When you realize you need to abandon yourself to God's will, Mother says:

> To know that the Father's Wisdom is in every cross is faith. To trust that everything that happens to us is for our good is hope. But to express our love for Him in the midst of darkness and aridity is the purest love.

9. When you feel you've sinned too much for God to love you still, Mother says:

> God always forgives when you are totally repentant and you desire to change. He forgives . . . and He never gets tired of forgiving. Never. You may get tired of asking. I hope not. He never, never tires of forgiving. Never.

10. When you're discerning the next step in life, Mother says:

> Unless you are willing to do the ridiculous, God will not do the miraculous. When you have God, you don't have to know everything about it; you just do it. . . . Everything starts with one person. . . . I don't care if you're 5 or 105, God from all eternity chose you to be where you are, at this time in history, to change the world.

If you have not read much by Mother Angelica or have not watched her shows, I highly recommend spending time with her. You will laugh, you will cry, and you will be inspired to grow in your love of God and become a great saint.

"The Lord God has no one else but you. You'd better get off your lead bottoms and go out there and change this pagan world!" (Mother Angelica)

PART 4

Prayers and Reflections on the Saints

21

Everyday Prayers and Litanies

For me, prayer is a surge of the heart; it is a simple look turned toward heaven, it is a cry of recognition and of love, embracing both trial and joy.[51]

—St. Thérèse of Lisieux

The following are traditional Catholic prayers as well as formulas for creating your own litanies. Pray them frequently and teach them to your children.

Morning Offering

O Jesus,
through the Immaculate Heart of Mary,
I offer You my prayers, works, joys, and sufferings
of this day,
for all the intentions of Thy Sacred Heart,
in union with the Holy Sacrifice of the Mass

[51] *The Story of a Soul*, chap. 5, quoted in the *Catechism of the Catholic Church*, no. 2558.

throughout the world,
in reparation for my sins,
for the intentions of all my relatives and friends,
and in particular for the intentions
of the Holy Father. Amen.

Angelus

V. The angel of the Lord declared unto Mary,
R. And she conceived of the Holy Spirit. Hail Mary . . .

V. Behold the handmaid of the Lord;
R. Be it done unto me according to your word. Hail Mary . . .

V. (Kneel) And the Word became Flesh
R. (Kneeling) And dwelt among us. Hail Mary . . .

V. Pray for us O Holy Mother of God,
R. That we may be made worthy of the promises of Christ.

V. Let us pray:

R. Pour forth, we beseech You, O Lord, Your grace into our hearts, that we, to whom the Incarnation of Christ, Your Son, was made known by the message of an angel, may by His Passion and Cross be brought to the glory of His Resurrection, through the same Christ Our Lord. Amen.

Regina Caeli (to be prayed in place of the Angelus during the Easter Season)

V. Queen of Heaven, rejoice, alleluia.
R. For He Whom you did merit to bear, alleluia.

V. Has risen, as He said, alleluia.
R. Pray for us to God, alleluia.

V. Rejoice and be glad, O Virgin Mary, alleluia.
R. For the Lord has truly risen, alleluia.

V. Let us pray:
R. O God, Who gave joy to the world through the Resurrection of Your Son, Our Lord Jesus Christ, grant, we beseech You, that through the intercession of the Virgin Mary, His Mother, we may obtain the joys of everlasting life. Through the same Christ Our Lord. Amen.

Divine Praises (to be prayed during Exposition and Benediction of the Most Blessed Sacrament or in thanksgiving at any time)

Blessed be God.
Blessed be His Holy Name.
Blessed be Jesus Christ, true God and true Man.
Blessed be the Name of Jesus.
Blessed be His Most Sacred Heart.
Blessed be His Most Precious Blood.
Blessed be Jesus in the Most Holy Sacrament of the Altar.
Blessed be the Holy Spirit, the Paraclete.
Blessed be the great Mother of God, Mary most holy.
Blessed be her holy and Immaculate Conception.
Blessed be her glorious Assumption.
Blessed be the name of Mary, Virgin and Mother.
Blessed be St. Joseph, her most chaste spouse.
Blessed be God in His angels and in His saints. Amen.

May the Heart of Jesus, in the Most Blessed Sacrament, be praised, adored, and loved with grateful affection, at every moment, in all the tabernacles of the world, even to the end of time. Amen.

Act of Spiritual Communion

My Jesus, I believe that You are present in the Most Holy Sacrament. I love You above all things, and I desire to receive You into my soul. Since I cannot at this moment receive You sacramentally, come at least spiritually into my heart. I embrace You as if You were already there and unite myself wholly to You. Never permit me to be separated from You. Amen.

Chaplet of Divine Mercy

Begin with the Sign of the Cross.
Pray once:

You expired, Jesus, but the source of life gushed forth for souls, and the ocean of mercy opened up for the whole world.

O Fount of Life, unfathomable Divine Mercy, envelop the whole world and empty Yourself out upon us.

Repeat thrice:

O Blood and Water, which gushed forth from the Heart of Jesus as a fount of mercy for us, I trust in You!

Using a rosary, begin with one Our Father, one Hail Mary, and the Apostles' Creed.
On the Our Father beads pray:

Eternal Father, I offer You the Body, Blood, Soul, and Divinity of Your dearly beloved Son, Our Lord Jesus Christ, in atonement for our sins and those of the whole world.

On the Hail Mary beads pray:

For the sake of His Sorrowful Passion, have mercy on us and on the whole world.

Repeat thrice:

Holy God, Holy Mighty One, Holy Immortal One, have mercy on us and on the whole world.

Conclude with the Sign of the Cross.

Chaplet of St. Michael

Begin with the Sign of the Cross.

O God, come to my assistance. O Lord, make haste to help me. Glory be …

After each of the following salutations, pray one Our Father and three Hail Marys.

- By the intercession of St. Michael and the celestial Choir of Seraphim, may the Lord make us worthy to burn with the fire of perfect charity. Our Father … Hail Mary …
- By the intercession of St. Michael and the celestial Choir of Cherubim, may the Lord grant us the grace to leave the ways of sin and run in the paths of Christian perfection.
- By the intercession of St. Michael and the celestial Choir of Thrones, may the Lord infuse into our hearts a true and sincere spirit of humility.
- By the intercession of St. Michael and the celestial Choir of Dominions, may the Lord give us the grace to govern our senses and overcome any unruly passions.

- By the intercession of St. Michael and the celestial Choir of Virtues, may the Lord preserve us from evil and falling into temptation.
- By the intercession of St. Michael and the celestial Choir of Powers, may the Lord protect our souls against the snares and temptations of the devil.
- By the intercession of St. Michael and the celestial Choir of Principalities, may God fill our souls with a true spirit of obedience.
- By the intercession of St. Michael and the celestial Choir of Archangels, may the Lord give us perseverance in faith and in all good works in order that we may attain the glory of Heaven.
- By the intercession of St. Michael and the celestial Choir of Angels, may the Lord grant us to be protected by them in this mortal life and conducted, in the life to come, to Heaven.

Pray one Our Father in honor of each of the following angels: St. Michael, St. Gabriel, St. Raphael, and your guardian angel.

O glorious prince St. Michael, chief and commander of the heavenly hosts, guardian of souls, vanquisher of rebel spirits, servant in the house of the Divine King and our admirable conductor, you who shine with excellence and superhuman virtue, deliver us from all evil, who turn to you with confidence, and enable us by your gracious protection to serve God more and more faithfully every day.

Pray for us, O glorious St. Michael, Prince of the Church of Jesus Christ, that we may be made worthy of His promises.

Almighty and Everlasting God, Who, by a prodigy of goodness and a merciful desire for the salvation of all men, has appointed the most glorious Archangel St. Michael Prince of Your Church, make us worthy, we ask You, to be delivered from all our enemies, that none of them may harass us at the hour of our death, but that we may be conducted by him into Your presence. We ask this through the merits of Jesus Christ Our Lord. Amen.

Litany of the Sacred Heart of Jesus

V. Lord, have mercy.
R. Lord, have mercy.
V. Christ, have mercy.
R. Christ, have mercy.
V. Lord, have mercy.
R. Lord, have mercy.
V. Christ, hear us.
R. Christ, hear us.
V. Christ, graciously hear us.
R. Christ, graciously hear us.
V. God, the Father of Heaven,
R. Have mercy on us.
God, the Son, Redeemer of the World …
God, the Holy Spirit …
Holy Trinity, one God …

Heart of Jesus, Son of the Eternal Father …

Heart of Jesus, formed by the Holy Spirit in the womb of the Virgin Mother …

Heart of Jesus, substantially united to the Word of God …
Heart of Jesus, of Infinite Majesty …
Heart of Jesus, Sacred Temple of God …
Heart of Jesus, Tabernacle of the Most High …
Heart of Jesus, House of God and Gate of Heaven …
Heart of Jesus, burning furnace of charity …
Heart of Jesus, abode of justice and love …
Heart of Jesus, full of goodness and love …
Heart of Jesus, abyss of all virtues …
Heart of Jesus, most worthy of all praise …
Heart of Jesus, King and center of all hearts …

Heart of Jesus, in Whom are all treasures of wisdom and knowledge …

Heart of Jesus, in Whom dwells the fullness of divinity …

Heart of Jesus, in Whom the Father was well pleased …

Heart of Jesus, of Whose fullness we have all received …

Heart of Jesus, desire of the everlasting hills …

Heart of Jesus, patient and most merciful …

Heart of Jesus, enriching all who invoke Thee …

Heart of Jesus, fountain of life and holiness …

Heart of Jesus, propitiation for our sins …

Heart of Jesus, loaded down with opprobrium …

Heart of Jesus, bruised for our offenses …

Heart of Jesus, obedient to death …

Heart of Jesus, pierced with a lance …

Heart of Jesus, source of all consolation …

Heart of Jesus, our life and resurrection …

Heart of Jesus, our peace and our reconciliation …

Heart of Jesus, victim for our sins …

Heart of Jesus, salvation of those who trust in You …

Heart of Jesus, hope of those who die in You …

Heart of Jesus, delight of all the saints …

V. Lamb of God, Who takes away the sins of the world,

R. Spare us, O Lord.

V. Lamb of God, Who takes away the sins of the world,

R. Graciously hear us, O Lord.

V. Lamb of God, Who takes away the sins of the world,

R. Have mercy on us, O Lord.

V. Jesus, meek and humble of heart,

R. Make our hearts like to Yours.

V. Let us pray:

R. Almighty and eternal God, look upon the Heart of Your Most Beloved Son and upon the praises and satisfaction which He offers You in the name of sinners; and to those who implore Your mercy, in Your great goodness, grant forgiveness in the Name of the same Jesus Christ, Your Son, Who lives and reigns with You forever and ever. Amen.

Litany of the Blessed Virgin Mary (Litany of Loreto)

V. Lord, have mercy.
R. Christ, have mercy.
V. Lord, have mercy on us. Christ, hear us.
R. Christ, graciously hear us.
V. God the Father of Heaven,
R. Have mercy on us.
V. God the Son, Redeemer of the world,
R. Have mercy on us.
V. God the Holy Spirit,
R. Have mercy on us.
V. Holy Trinity, One God,
R. Have mercy on us.

V. Holy Mary,
R. Pray for us.
Holy Mother of God …
Holy Virgin of virgins …
Mother of Christ …
Mother of the Church …
Mother of Mercy …
Mother of Divine Grace …

Mother of Hope …
Mother most pure …
Mother most chaste …
Mother inviolate …
Mother undefiled …
Mother most amiable …
Mother admirable …
Mother of good counsel …
Mother of our Creator …
Mother of our Savior …
Virgin most prudent …
Virgin most venerable …
Virgin most renowned …
Virgin most powerful …
Virgin most merciful …
Virgin most faithful …
Mirror justice …
Seat of wisdom …
Cause of our joy …
Spiritual vessel …
Vessel of honor …
Singular vessel of devotion …
Mystical Rose …
Tower of David …
Tower of ivory …
House of gold …
Ark of the Covenant …
Gate of Heaven …
Morning star …
Health of the sick …
Refuge of sinners …

Solace of migrants ...
Comfort of the afflicted ...
Help of Christians ...
Queen of Angels ...
Queen of Patriarchs ...
Queen of Prophets ...
Queen of Apostles ...
Queen of Martyrs ...
Queen of Confessors ...
Queen of Virgins ...
Queen of All Saints ...
Queen conceived without Original Sin ...
Queen assumed into Heaven ...
Queen of the Most Holy Rosary ...
Queen of families ...
Queen of peace ...

V. Lamb of God, Who takes away the sins of the world,
R. Spare us, O Lord.
V. Lamb of God, Who takes away the sins of the world,
R. Graciously hear us, O Lord.
V. Lamb of God, Who takes away the sins of the world,
R. Have mercy on us.
V. Pray for us, O Holy Mother of God,
R. That we may be made worthy of the promises of Christ.

V. Let us pray:

R. Grant, we beseech You, O Lord God, that we, your servants, may enjoy perpetual health of mind and body, and by the glorious intercession of the Blessed Mary, ever Virgin, may be delivered from present sorrow, and obtain eternal joy. Through Christ Our Lord. Amen.

Litany of St. Joseph

V. Lord, have mercy.
R. Christ, have mercy.
V. Lord, have mercy on us. Christ, hear us.
R. Christ, graciously hear us.
V. God the Father of Heaven,
R. Have mercy on us.
V. God the Son, Redeemer of the World,
R. Have mercy on us.
V. God the Holy Spirit,
R. Have mercy on us.
V. Holy Trinity, One God,
R. Have mercy on us.

V. Holy Mary,
R. Pray for us.
St. Joseph …
Renowned offspring of David …
Light of Patriarchs …
Spouse of the Mother of God …
Chaste guardian of the Virgin …
Foster father of the Son of God …
Diligent protector of Christ …
Head of the Holy Family …
Joseph most just …
Joseph most chaste …
Joseph most prudent …
Joseph most strong …
Joseph most obedient …
Joseph most faithful …
Mirror of patience …

Lover of poverty …
Model of artisans …
Glory of home life …
Guardian of virgins …
Pillar of families …
Solace of the wretched …
Hope of the sick …
Patron of the dying …
Terror of demons …
Protector of Holy Church …

V. Lamb of God, Who takes away the sins of the world,
R. Spare us, O Jesus.
V. Lamb of God, Who takes away the sins of the world,
R. Graciously hear us, O Jesus.
V. Lamb of God, Who takes away the sins of the world,
R. Have mercy on us, O Jesus.
V. He made him the lord of his household
R. And prince over all his possessions.

V. Let us pray:

R. O God, in Your ineffable Providence, You were pleased to choose Blessed Joseph to be the spouse of Your most holy Mother; grant, we beg You, that we may be worthy to have him for our intercessor in Heaven whom on earth we venerate as our protector: You who live and reign forever and ever. Amen.

Litany of the Tired Parent (by the Cowdens)

V. Lord, have mercy.
R. Christ, have mercy.
V. Lord, have mercy on us. Christ, hear us.
R. Christ, graciously hear us.

V. God the Father of Heaven,
R. Have mercy on us.
V. God the Son, Redeemer of the World,
R. Have mercy on us.
V. God the Holy Spirit,
R. Have mercy on us.
V. Holy Trinity, One God,
R. Have mercy on us.

V. Holy Mary,
R. Pray for us.
St. Joseph …
Holy angels …
Blessed saints …

V. From the evil of sin,
R. Deliver us, Jesus.
From the temptations around us …
From the glamour of the world …
From the distractions that abound …
From the deadly sin of pride …
From the deadly sin of greed …
From the deadly sin of lust …
From the deadly sin of envy …
From the deadly sin of gluttony …
From the deadly sin of wrath …
From the deadly sin of sloth …

V. For the will to seek You in all things,
R. Jesus, grant me the grace to desire it.
For the will to prefer Your ways over ours …
For the will to spend more time with You …
For the will to emulate the heroic virtue of the saints …

For the will to root out vice …
For the will to remain in union with You …
For the will to raise our children in the Faith …
For the will to orient our day around You …
For the will to make difficult decisions for our family …
For the will to be faithful …
For the will to be hopeful …
For the will to be charitable …
For the will to be patient …
For the will to be gentle …
For the will to be empathetic …
For the will to be merciful …
For the will to be generous …
For the will to choose virtue at all times …
For the will to be steadfast …
For the will to grow in love of You …

V. Lamb of God, Who takes away the sins of the world,
R. Spare us, O Lord.
V. Lamb of God, Who takes away the sins of the world,
R. Graciously hear us, O Lord.
V. Lamb of God, Who takes away the sins of the world,
R. Have mercy on us, O Lord.

V. Jesus, meek and humble of heart,
R. Make our hearts like to Thine.

V. Let us pray:
R: Lord, Who gave us the beautiful vocation of marriage and the gift of our children: Grant that we might always seek to do Your will, to follow the example of the saints, and to persevere in faith, that we might enjoy eternal Paradise with you forever in Heaven. Amen.

22

Reflections on Saints for Catholic Parents

"You have a patron saint for everything, don't you!"

A dear friend of ours made this lighthearted exclamation while at our house one day, as I was going on about the many amazing saints of our Catholic Faith. She's right: there's a patron saint for every cause. Whatever the trials we're facing, whatever the crosses we're carrying, there is at least one saint in our Church's two-thousand-year history to whom we can relate.

Here are reflections and prayers that will help you befriend these saints, who have faced illnesses, persecutions, poverty, deaths of loved ones, and other tremendous obstacles. Let us look to them often for guidance and hope, asking for their intercession.

Included with each reflection is a prayer and what the Cowdens call a "passing prayer." We highly recommend memorizing the passing prayers as you need them, as well as coming up with your own spontaneous passing prayers.

All ye holy men and women, pray for us!

The Blessed Mother and a Prayer for a Mother

FIRST CENTURY AD • FEAST DAY: JANUARY 1 • PATRONESS OF ALL HUMANITY

I am the handmaid of the Lord. Let it be done unto me according to thy word.

Luke 1:38, DR

They say moms can do it all, and the Blessed Mother, without a doubt, is the gold standard for motherhood. Patroness of all humanity and mother of us all, she's always here to help us, if only we ask her!

I don't know about you, but I ask for her help frequently during the day. Not a day goes by when I don't talk to "Mama Mary," and not just through praying the Rosary but in little moments throughout the day. As I'm preparing food for the kids, changing diapers, nursing the baby, breaking up squabbles, trying to get work done for my full-time job, or staring at the looming mountain of laundry that needs to be folded, I ask the Blessed Mother to help me to be a better wife and mother.

I want so badly to be more like the Blessed Mother—to possess her patience, her gentleness, and her love of her Son. But I know that, more often than not, I fall short. I snap at the kids and my husband. I yell sometimes. I don't always behave the way I would if Jesus were in the room with me. Yes, I *know* He's always there, but obviously, I don't act like it!

When I talk to Mary throughout the day, I'm face-to-face with the Mother of Mercy, the Mother of Divine Grace, the Mother of Hope, and the Mother of Good Counsel, as she's titled in the Litany of Loreto. I'm directly asking the best mother in the history of mankind to be with me and show me her ways.

Talking to Mary throughout the day makes a mother's days more manageable. When a mother has her own heavenly Mother nearby, her Mother who knows the joys and sorrows of parenting, she doesn't feel alone. She can offer her shortcomings and her struggles to the Blessed Mother to place at the feet of her Son. With the help of Our Lady, every moment of a mother's day can be a prayer.

Not only should a mother pray continually to the Blessed Mother, but her family should pray for her too. Here's a short prayer for mothers that fathers and children can pray to give mothers strength throughout the day.

Let us pray:

For mothers to pray:

Blessed Mother Mary, cover me with your mantle of love.
Help me to be patient.
Help me to be productive.
Help me to be joyful.
Help me to be present.
Help me to be prayerful.
Help me to be gentle.
Help me to be more like you,
Through your Son, Jesus Christ, Our Lord. Amen.

For fathers and children to pray:

Blessed Mother Mary, cover Mom with your mantle of love.
Help her to be patient.
Help her to be productive.
Help her to be joyful.
Help her to be present.
Help her to be prayerful.
Help her to be gentle.
Help her to be more like you,
Through your Son, Jesus Christ, Our Lord. Amen.

Passing Prayer

Blessed Mother Mary, cover Mom with your mantle of love.
Help her to be more like you. Amen.

St. Joseph and a Prayer of a Father

FIRST CENTURY AD • FEAST DAY: MARCH 19 • PATRON OF FATHERS, A HAPPY DEATH, AND THE UNIVERSAL CHURCH

There are many saints to whom God has given the power to assist in the necessities of life, but the power given to St. Joseph is unlimited: It extends to all our needs, and all those who invoke him with confidence are sure to be heard.[52]

—St. Thomas Aquinas

Can you believe that, in the two thousand years of our Church's history, we are just now coming to a greater recognition of the foster father of Jesus? Only in the last 150 years have St. Joseph's life and spirituality been examined more deeply.

St. Joseph never speaks a word in Scripture, yet his life is a treasure trove for spiritual meditation. He shows men how to love chastely, work diligently, and act courageously, even in the face of the evil that sought to destroy his family.

In the recent Year of St. Joseph, Catholic families have taken up with new fervor the exhortation "*Ite ad Joseph!*" (Go to St. Joseph!) and have developed a new fondness for our spiritual father.

[52] Quoted in Rev. Nicholas O'Rafferty, *Discourses on St. Joseph* (Milwaukee: Bruce, 1951), 208.

Second to God the Father, St. Joseph is the best example of who and what a father should strive to be. Therefore, it makes sense to strive to be like him in every way.

Men, as we continue to "go to Joseph" as husbands and fathers, let us ask for his help in all areas of our lives.

Let us pray:

St. Joseph, you embody all the virtues I hope to attain through God's grace. I rely on your intercession and your guidance as I strive for holiness for myself and my family.

Adopt me as your spiritual son, so that I might learn from you.

Train me to hear God's voice and discern His will, you who heard God even while sleeping.

Take me to Egypt with you, along with my family, and protect us from the evil that wishes to harm us.

Help me to model purity and chastity for my family, that my children might be truly free to embrace God's vocation for them.

Show me how to exercise patience, that I might overcome my frustrations and embrace suffering.

Teach me holy silence, that my mind and my heart might be attuned to the presence of Jesus, especially in the Eucharist.

Lead me always to Jesus, that I might be able to gaze upon His Holy Face, in all its radiance, for all eternity.

I beg you, O glorious St. Joseph, to present my intentions before your Son, who always defers to you in holy obedience. Amen.

Passing Prayer

St. Joseph, adopt me as your spiritual son, so that I might learn from you. Amen.

The Holy Archangels and a Prayer for the Protection of the Angels

FEAST DAY: SEPTEMBER 29 • PATRONS OF POLICE AND THE MILITARY (ST. MICHAEL); OF JOURNALISTS AND COMMUNICATION (ST. GABRIEL); OF PHYSICIANS, NURSES, AND TRAVELERS (ST. RAPHAEL)

> *The battle against the devil, which is the principal task of St. Michael the Archangel, is still being fought today because the devil is still alive and active in the world.*[53]
>
> —Pope St. John Paul II

In our home, the archangel whose intercession we most frequently implore is St. Michael, through the familiar prayer to him. The presence of evil in the world is palpable. It's as though the devil enjoys rearing his ugly head because he knows sin is glorified by our society.

You can understand, then, the reason for praying to St. Michael daily. Sometimes I pray to him three or four times a day. Encourage

[53] Said during a visit to the Sanctuary of St. Michael the Archangel, May 24, 1987.

your children to pray to St. Michael for protection, especially when they're tempted or scared.

This is the Prayer to St. Michael given to us by Pope Leo XIII in 1884:

> St. Michael the Archangel, defend us in battle! Be our protection against the wickedness and snares of the devil. May God rebuke him, we humbly pray, and do thou, O Prince of the Heavenly Host, by the power of God, cast into Hell Satan and all the evil spirits who prowl about the world seeking the ruin of souls. Amen.

Besides providing protection, the archangels are perfect examples of obedience to God and His plans for our lives. Each, in his own way, contributes to the salvation of mankind:

- St. Michael is the leader of all the holy angels, and he cast Satan and his minions into Hell for all eternity.
- St. Gabriel announced the birth of John the Baptist to his father, Zechariah, and announced the Incarnation to the Blessed Virgin Mary.
- St. Raphael healed Tobias's blindness in the Old Testament and is recognized as a conduit of God's healing and mercy.

Oh, how much better the world would be if we all glorified God as these archangels do! Whereas droves of evil spirits were expelled from Heaven for their disobedience, these archangels have been honored for their obedience.

Today and every day, let us choose obedience and faithfulness to God's will, with the help of the archangels.

Let us pray:

O powerful archangels, Sts. Michael, Gabriel, and Raphael, come to my assistance today.

St. Michael, help me to resist the empty promises of the devil and to fight for the glory of God's Kingdom.

St. Gabriel, help me to be attuned to God's voice and to live my vocation according to His will.

St. Raphael, help me to be open to the graces given to me in the sacraments, and cover me with the healing power of our mighty God.

Faithful archangels, do not leave my side. Amen.

Passing Prayer

Powerful archangels, do not leave my side. Amen.

St. Gianna Molla and a Prayer for Married Couples

1922–1962 • FEAST DAY: APRIL 28 •
PATRON OF MOTHERS, WIVES, UNBORN CHILDREN, AND FAMILIES

It is not right to come to the Lord without enough suffering.[54]

—St. Gianna Molla

When I was in eighth grade, I was preparing to choose a Confirmation saint. I was all but set on St. Cecilia, in honor of my love of music, when I learned of St. Gianna Beretta Molla, who had been canonized the year before. I didn't feel as though I had anything in common with her, but something drew me to her. Maybe it was the thrill of being able to pick a brand-new saint for my Confirmation name.

Little did I know that she chose me. As I grew in my Faith during high school, I became stronger in my pro-life convictions. St. Gianna is a patron of unborn children because she bravely chose life for her unborn daughter, even though her own life was in danger. Having been diagnosed with a uterine fibroid during a pregnancy, she was urged to have a hysterectomy, which would have caused an abortion. St. Gianna refused, saying, "If you must

[54] Quoted in Molla, *Saint Gianna Molla*, 87.

decide between me and the child, do not hesitate: choose the child—I insist on it." She died a week after delivering a healthy baby girl by cesarean section.

While learning more about St. Gianna's life—her career as a doctor, her involvement in the St. Vincent de Paul Society, and her enthusiasm for skiing, mountain climbing, and painting—I became fascinated by the relationship she had with her husband, Pietro. From friendship to courtship, to engagement, and throughout their marriage, their love was one of trust, faithfulness, and admiration. I wanted a marriage like that.

In college, I began dating Dave, who had chosen St. Joseph as his Confirmation saint. My future husband's patron was the patron of fathers, while mine was that of mothers. Together, we prayed for their intercession as we discerned marriage. The more I dated Dave and the closer we got to marriage, the more I realized we were headed toward a love like the one Pietro and Gianna had.

And our prayers to St. Gianna didn't stop on our wedding day. A few days before the 2015 World Meeting of Families, we discovered I was pregnant. While in Philadelphia producing EWTN's live coverage, I met Dr. Gianna Emanuela Molla, the daughter of St. Gianna—the daughter whose life was saved by her mother's selfless act of love. I choked back tears as I told her we intended to name our first daughter after her mom, who had already been so generous in interceding for us. Dr. Molla replied, "It brings me so much joy to hear how people benefit from the prayers of my mother in Heaven!" Less than a year later, I was with Dr. Molla again and introduced her to my newborn daughter, Gianna.

And do you think the prayers to St. Gianna stopped after I gave birth to our own Gianna? Absolutely not. Having been a modern-day mother, St. Gianna knows the struggles we're facing. Having been a working mother of three, with a fourth on the way, she understands the unique challenges that come with trying to find a balance between work and family life. She, too, tried to orient her life, her marriage, and her family toward Heaven—to the extent that she didn't hesitate to save her child's life, even if her earthly life ended as a result. Since the Church has declared that she is numbered among the saints in Heaven, we can rest assured that she's helping us as we try to attain our heavenly reward too.

I *love* St. Gianna, and it is my prayer that more mothers (and fathers) grow in their devotion to this wonderful and imitable mother.

Let us pray:

St. Gianna Molla, you modeled extraordinary love for your husband, your children, and God, and I'm leaning on you today to help me with my struggles. (*State your intention.*) I want to embrace the joys and sufferings of marriage and parenting, but I need help. Pray that I might grow to love my spouse and children more and more each day and that I will bear these burdens bravely and faithfully, as you did unto death. Amen.

Passing Prayer

St. Gianna Molla, pray that I will bear these burdens faithfully and bravely, as you did unto death. Amen.

Sts. Joachim and Anne and a Prayer of Couples Struggling with Infertility

FIRST CENTURY AD • FEAST DAY: JULY 26 • PATRONS OF COUPLES SUFFERING WITH INFERTILITY

Anne is the blessed barren woman, happy mother among mothers, from whose pure womb came forth the shining temple of God, the sanctuary of the Holy Ghost, the Mother of God![55]

—St. Jerome

Infertility. It's a cross that many couples carry silently. If you or someone close to you carries it, I don't have to tell you how heavy the cross is. Though there appears to be less and less stigma associated with infertility nowadays, it's still a deeply personal and agonizing journey for the couples who experience it.

God, in His goodness, has given us saints who have carried this cross too. Sts. Joachim and Anne, the parents of the Blessed Virgin Mary, experienced infertility. Said to be barren in their old age, they knew firsthand the pain of infertility but didn't lose faith in God. In fact, the opposite is true. They doubled down

[55] *Good Saint Anne* (Clyde, MO: Benedictine Convent of Perpetual Adoration, 1958).

and increased their prayer and fasting. Though they were grieved, they didn't give up.

And the Lord blessed them. Tradition tells us an angel appeared to them, saying, "The Lord has heard your prayer" and prophesying about their child's role in salvation history.

This is not a promise to us that if we pray hard enough, God will cure infertility. But the Lord hears our prayers. If you suffer from infertility, know that God loves you and that this cross will bring forth fruit.

In times of desperate prayer, Dave and I have found that the more we pray, the more our hearts become attuned to God's will. It's as though, through our prayers, we are transformed and enlightened about God's will for our lives.

Sometimes it's the suffering that draws us closer to God. Sometimes it's the pain of hearing no after no after no that primes our hearts for the eventual yes. Sometimes the yes we receive isn't even the yes we originally prayed for. It's even better.

The years of disappointment of Sts. Joachim and Anne are a reminder to us that God is at work, even when we don't see the immediate fruits of our prayers. While they were recalling the story of Abraham and Sarah, and how God answered their prayers, Sts. Joachim and Anne couldn't possibly have imagined how great God's plan was for them.

Pray the following prayer together, and often. While praying it, believe in God's goodness and His amazing plan for your life.

Let us pray:

God, we know that You are faithful. We know that You are loving. We know that You are all-powerful and all-good. We praise You for Your goodness. We praise You for Your compassion. We praise You for Your generosity. Through the intercession of Sts. Joachim and Anne, who saw Your generosity firsthand, we beg You to answer our prayers for (*Name*). May we, like Sts. Joachim and Anne, always be docile to Your plan and obedient to Your divine will, forever and ever. Amen.

Passing Prayer

Through the intercession of Sts. Joachim and Anne, Lord, we ask You to hear our prayers as we strive to conform to Your will. Amen.

Sts. Joachim and Anne and a Prayer for Grandparents

FIRST CENTURY AD • FEAST DAY: JULY 26 • PATRONS OF GRANDPARENTS

Joachim and Anne, how blessed a couple! All creation is indebted to you. For at your hands the Creator was offered a gift excelling all other gifts: a chaste mother, who alone was worthy of him.[56]

—St. John Damascene

If you've ever shopped for gifts for grandparents, you've undoubtedly seen the kitschy phrase "The Best Parents Get Promoted to Grandparents" or "The Best Dads Get Promoted to Grandpa" or something similar.

No doubt, Sts. Joachim and Anne were special. From the beginning of the Blessed Virgin Mary's life, they took special care to protect Mary and to raise her to love God. They brought her to the Temple to be blessed and consecrated. It appears they did everything right as parents.

It only makes sense that they would be promoted to grandparents of the Son of God! There aren't many details about the relationship, if any, that Joachim and Anne had with the Child

[56] From a sermon of St. John Damascene, in *Liturgy of the Hours*, Office of Readings, July 26.

Jesus. But based on the care with which they raised the Virgin Mary, it is reasonable to suggest they would have done the same with their Grandson.

What we know is that, based on their role in bearing and raising the Mother of God, they must have been holy, righteous, and obedient. They must have known and practiced the Jewish faith in order to raise Mary in a godly manner. They laid the foundation upon which the Divine Child Jesus could learn the faith too.

Grandparents today have this same responsibility—not only to play with the grandkids (and occasionally offer their free services as babysitters—am I right?) but also to raise the grandchildren in the Faith: to teach them virtue, to pray with them, to pass along the stories of the saints and our Catholic heritage, and, in a bittersweet way, to show their children and grandchildren how to prepare for a happy, holy death.

Let's not forget that they need additional prayers for a variety of other reasons—for their health and wellness, for their safety, that they might not experience loneliness, and the many other unique needs of our elderly loved ones.

We offer this prayer for grandparents. Pray it together regularly as a family and encourage your children to add their specific intentions for their grandmas and grandpas.

Let us pray:

> O God, we praise You and thank You for the gift of our grandparents, (*Names*). We are thankful for their wisdom, for their love, and for all the memories we've been able to make together. We ask you to watch over them this day, that they might be healthy, happy, and holy, and (*mention any other intentions*). We pray that, through the intercession of Sts. Joachim and Anne, they might enjoy the final years of

their lives and, at the hour of their death, may be welcomed into Heaven to be with You forever. Amen.

Passing Prayer

God, thank You for the gift of our grandparents. Watch over them so they might be healthy, happy, and holy. Amen.

St. Monica and a Prayer for the Conversion of Family Members

AD 331–387 • FEAST DAY: AUGUST 27 • PATRON OF MOTHERS

Nothing is far to God.[57]

—St. Monica

We all know someone who has left the Faith. Are you praying for that person's return?

St. Monica is remembered and lauded for her spiritual endurance as she prayed for the conversion of her husband, Patricius, and her son Augustine. Her prayers, which went on for years, were finally answered. Patricius converted a year before his death, and Augustine went on to become one of the greatest saints in the Church.

It's not easy to persevere in prayer, and it *is* easy to give up on those who have left the Faith. St. Monica knew the struggles. At first, she shunned Augustine, who had joined a heretical cult. He left her without notice to travel to Rome. He fathered a child out of wedlock. Augustine admitted to Monica that he would work toward healing the relationship if she would leave her Faith.

[57] Quoted in St. Augustine, *Confessions*, bk. 9, chap. 11, par. 28.

Grief and worry plagued Monica, but they did not overcome her. She continued to pray and sought advice from bishops and clergy on how to help her son. One local bishop assured her, "It is not possible that the son of such tears shall perish."[58]

God sees the tears we shed for our wayward loved ones. He hears the prayers and the pleading. When we don't immediately get the answer we seek, let us look to St. Monica for strength to continue praying. As it turns out, Monica's years of praying resulted not only in the sanctity of her son but in her own sanctity.

Let us pray:

St. Monica, you persevered in prayer for your husband and your son, though it appeared to the world they were beyond the Lord's reach. I ask you to pray alongside me for the conversion of (*Name*). O faithful St. Monica, pray for my loved one as you prayed for St. Augustine. Amen.

Passing Prayer

O faithful St. Monica, pray for my loved one as you prayed for St. Augustine. Amen.

[58] Ibid., bk. 3, chap. 12, par. 21.

St. Rita and a Prayer for an Impossible Cause

1381–1457 • FEAST DAY: MAY 22 • PATRON OF IMPOSSIBLE CAUSES, ABUSE VICTIMS, MARITAL PROBLEMS, AND BODILY WOUNDS

Let me, my Jesus, share in Thy suffering, at least one of Thy thorns.[59]

—St. Rita of Cascia

St. Rita had a hard life. She was married at age twelve to a reportedly violent man, who was murdered eighteen years later in a family feud. Her twin sons sought revenge on their father's killer, and both ended up dying of dysentery. She attempted to join a convent but was refused because of her family's history and her husband's violent death. She received the stigmata. She died of tuberculosis after being bedridden for the last four years of her life.

If there's anyone you can turn to during difficult, seemingly impossible, times, it's St. Rita.

Through the hardships she endured throughout her life, she persevered in faith. She embraced her sufferings. She continued praying. She responded to wrongdoings with forgiveness.

[59] Quoted in "St. Rita of Cascia," Catholic Culture, https://www.catholicculture.org/culture/liturgicalyear/calendar/day.cfm?date=2006-05-22.

When we pray for the intercession of the "saint of impossible causes," we might ask to have the impossible situation alleviated, to have the problem go away. Instead, what if we approached our impossible causes as St. Rita did, asking for the grace to face the painful situation courageously, to respond virtuously, and to remain faithful to God?

What if we, like St. Rita, delighted in the chance to share in the sufferings of Christ? Wow! That would change everything.

In the midst of your impossible cause, know that you have a heavenly friend who knows your struggles and is praying for you to persevere in love.

Let us pray:

St. Rita, I come before you with a problem that feels impossible, a cause that seems lost. I don't know how this situation is going to turn out, and I'm struggling to (*find peace, keep the faith, remain patient, feel God's presence, etc.*). You are no stranger to suffering, and you were able to conform to the will of God, no matter what. Help me to bear this suffering, this thorn, with joy and love, so that I, too, may conform to God's loving will. Amen.

Passing Prayer

St. Rita, help me to bear this suffering, this thorn, with joy and love. Amen.

St. Elizabeth of Portugal and a Prayer for the Healing of Family Rifts

1271–1336 • FEAST DAY: JULY 4 • PATRON FOR HEALING OF FAMILY RIFTS

If you love peace, all will be well.[60]

—St. Elizabeth of Portugal

It's safe to say that every family has its share of drama, from waywardness to personality clashes to sibling rivalry, and so on. Some families experience deep wounds that cause seemingly irreconcilable conflict. Some hurts seem unforgivable.

Even the saints had family drama. That's why we can look to holy examples such as St. Elizabeth of Portugal, who, as queen, on two known occasions, prevented her kingdom from entering a civil war. She literally stood between the two armies of her quarreling husband and son and was able to assist them in making peace.

Have any of our family feuds resulted in the assembling of literal armies? No, I don't think so!

But that doesn't mean that our personal battles aren't legitimate. After all, we know that the devil loves seeing the destruction of

[60] Quoted in Enzo Lodi, *Saints of the Roman Calendar*, trans. Jordan Aumann, O.P. (Staten Island, NY: Society of St. Paul, 2012), 175.

the family, the domestic church. If the family breaks down, it's easier for him to win souls for Hell.

St. Elizabeth was familiar with this. While other members of her family and the royal court were engaging in immoral activities, she kept her eyes laser-focused on the Gospel and on her commitment to serving the poor. Not only was she a peacemaker in her family, but she also modeled virtue for those around her.

The prayer below would be wonderful to adopt during family strife. How can we continue fighting among ourselves when we take a moment to stop and pray? That's easier said than done, I know. But if we truly want to heal family rifts and end "civil wars" in our families, the best way to initiate "peace talks" is through prayer.

Let us pray:

St. Elizabeth, you know all too well the pain of family rifts. You worked for peace within your family. We ask you to come to our aid as we pray for (*state your need*). Help us to seek peace as you did, to speak with kindness, and to work toward reconciliation; and above all, help us to love God through loving one another more. Amen.

Passing Prayer

St. Elizabeth of Portugal, help us to heal our family rifts. Amen.

St. Anthony of Padua and a Prayer for a Lost Soul

1195–1231 • FEAST DAY: JUNE 13 • PATRON OF LOST ITEMS, LOST SOULS, THE ELDERLY, THE OPPRESSED, THE POOR, AND MORE

Each saint in heaven rejoices over the glorification of the other, and his love overflows to him.... The same joy will fill all the blessed, for I shall rejoice over your well-being as though it were my own, and you will rejoice over mine as though it were yours.[61]

—St. Anthony of Padua

St. Anthony of Padua is one of the greatest and most recognizable saints in the Church. Unfortunately, he tends to get pigeonholed as "the patron saint of lost objects," the one who finds your stuff when you think you've looked everywhere. You've heard the jingle: "Good Saint Anthony, come around. Something's lost and can't be found." That's fine, but there's so much more to this great saint. He is also the patron of lost souls, the elderly, those who love the Blessed Sacrament, amputees, the poor, the oppressed, pregnant women, hostesses, those who are sterile or barren, people who are starving, and more!

[61] Patrick McCloskey, O.F.M., *St. Anthony of Padua: Wisdom for Today* (Cincinnati: Franciscan Media, 1986).

St. Anthony was an amazing preacher and teacher, a kindred spirit of St. Francis of Assisi, a miracle-worker, and the father of mystical theology. And he was affectionately referred to as "the Hammer of Heretics." You can see why my husband and I named our son after him!

And as he's commonly portrayed holding the Child Jesus, there's not a doubt in my mind that he has the ear of our Savior.

Instead of only invoking St. Anthony's intercession for help in finding a lost item, try asking for his assistance in recovering a "lost soul"—that is, someone who has left the Faith or who has been far from the Faith. You can offer this prayer for someone you know or someone you don't know. Imagine the greeting you'll receive in Heaven when you're approached by someone you prayed for. What a joy it is to be a member of the Body of Christ!

Let us pray:

O Holy St. Anthony, Hammer of Heretics, miracle-worker, and Doctor of the Church, you humbly lived your life in service of Christ, preaching truth in charity at a time when heresy persisted. St. Anthony, patron of lost souls, I ask you to keep in mind a particular lost soul (*Name*), who I fear is in danger of eternal punishment. O devotee of the Child Jesus, bring my prayer before Our Lord, that (*Name*) might be protected from harm and reconciled with our merciful Father. Amen.

Passing Prayer

St. Anthony, patron of lost souls, intercede for the conversion of (*Name*), who is in danger of eternal loss. Amen.

St. Thérèse of Lisieux and a Prayer of a Parent during a Child's Tantrum

1873–1897 • FEAST DAY: OCTOBER 1 • PATRON OF MISSIONARIES, FLORISTS, HOMELESS PEOPLE, AND ORPHANED CHILDREN

He . . . gave me to understand that my own glory wouldn't be apparent to mortal eyes, that it would consist in becoming a great Saint! . . . This desire might seem foolhardy if one were to consider how weak and imperfect I was, and how much I still am after seven years spent in the religious life, but nonetheless I still feel the same audacious confidence that I'll become a great Saint. That's because I'm not counting on my merits, since I have none, but I hope in the One who is Virtue and Holiness Itself.[62]

—St. Thérèse of Lisieux

When children are in the midst of full-blown temper tantrums, it's hard to see them as saints in the making. Even our eldest, who never really went through the "terrible twos" (praise God!), still has her occasional meltdowns. These are not fun for anyone, and

[62] Quoted in *The Complete Thérèse of Lisieux* (Brewster, MA: Paraclete Press, 2009), 59.

they're not usually times when we think about loving God and helping our children become saints.

In one of her letters to her husband, St. Zélie Martin said of her three-year-old daughter, Thérèse, "I have to correct this poor baby, who goes into a terrible rage when things don't go as she'd like. She rolls around on the floor like a desperate person, believing all is lost."[63]

As much as we hate to admit it, tantrums are a normal part of childhood. A child's brain is still growing and developing, meaning it's nearly impossible for a child to react or respond to situations in the way adults do.

While this is not a parenting book, I have to share with you the biggest game-changer in parenting for our family. When our kids are melting down, no matter the reason, we hug them.

If our little Anthony is screaming, hitting his sisters, and throwing toys, and he seems inconsolable, I kneel down, hug him, and tell him I love him. When we can step away from the conflict for a moment, he can tell me, "Momma, I'm so frustrated. Gigi knocked down my tower!" and we can calmly address the situation.

There have been a few occasions when Gianna was completely melting down for what seemed like no reason. After hugging her and asking some questions, we discovered that the source of the frustration was hunger or thirst or the need to go to the bathroom. Who would have thought? Yes, she could have simply told me she needed to go to the bathroom, but anyone who has kids knows it's not always that easy.

When we started taking this approach, we found that our kids' tantrums subsided almost immediately. Our kids recognized that

[63] *A Call to Deeper Love*, Letter 147.

we loved them and were there for them. Who doesn't love a good hug when things have gone sour?

We also started asking St. Thérèse to help us through the tantrums. This simple prayer that we can say in the midst of conflict and strong emotions allows children to experience firsthand the benefit of the intercession of the saints.

Yes, dealing with tantrums is hard. I've had to overcome my inclination to yell and punish my kids. And I've messed up and yelled.

But we love our kids so much, don't we? We desire their holiness. We desire a good relationship with them. Most of us need a little help overcoming our own vices so we can help our children grow in virtue.

St. Thérèse's parents loved her through her tantrums, and we can love our kids through theirs too. Let's ask St. Thérèse of Lisieux to remind us of our call to love God in the small ways of parenting.

Let us pray:

St. Thérèse, you know well the ups and downs of family life. You know that families are not perfect and that we sometimes resort to yelling and fighting. You also know that the family is the school of love, in which we learn charity, forgiveness, and self-control. Help me in the midst of this trial. Show me how to love God through my child. Help me to be patient, gentle, and compassionate. May this tantrum bring my child and me one step closer to Heaven. Amen.

Passing Prayer

St. Thérèse, show me how to love God through my child. Help me to be patient, gentle, and compassionate. Amen.

St. Josemaría Escrivá and a Prayer for the Person Who "Sanctifies" You

1902–1975 • FEAST DAY: JUNE 26 • PATRON OF OPUS DEI AND PEOPLE WITH DIABETES

Don't say, "That person gets on my nerves."
Think, "That person sanctifies me."[64]

—St. Josemaría Escrivá

Do you have people who "get on your nerves"? Of course you do. We all do. But if you're trying to grow in love of God and get your family to Heaven, you're going to have to change the way you think about those people.

St. Josemaría Escrivá is a perfect saint to go to for help in our everyday journey toward holiness. He was a priest who founded Opus Dei, a global apostolate that helps Catholics answer the call to ordinary holiness. He taught that everything we do must be for the glory of God.

That means that even our interactions with others must be for the glory of God.

[64] *The Way*, no. 174, Josemaría Escrivá, https://www.escrivaworks.org/book/the_way-point-174.htm.

So when someone is bothering you, offending you, inconveniencing you, or otherwise "getting on your nerves," you're given a golden opportunity to grow in holiness.

How, you ask?

You can take it as a sign that you need to grow in the virtues of kindness, humility, patience, self-control, generosity, gratitude, and so on. You can exercise those virtues, and perhaps it will rub off on the person whose behavior is affecting you. And you can *pray* for that person!

I assure you, if you can change the way you view your interactions with certain people, and if you see the opportunity to grow in holiness, your soul will rise to new heights!

Let us pray:

St. Josemaría Escrivá, you said it perfectly: "This person sanctifies me." Help me not to be bothered by this interaction, but help me to soften my heart so I can be sanctified. Remind me that everything I do should be oriented toward growing in holiness and getting to Heaven. Amen.

Passing Prayer

St. Josemaría Escrivá, help me to soften my heart so I can be sanctified by this interaction. Amen.

St. Isidore the Farmer & Bl. Maria Torribia and a Prayer in Thanksgiving for Groceries

1079–1172; D. 1175 • FEAST DAY: MAY 15 AND SEPTEMBER 15 • PATRONS OF FARMERS AND RURAL COMMUNITIES

Rejoice always, pray constantly, give thanks in all circumstances; for this is the will of God in Christ Jesus for you.

—1 Thessalonians 5:16–18

When was the last time you thanked God for your groceries? Or when was the last time you thanked God for the following:

- the people who work at the grocery store
- the truckers who freight your food across the country
- the farmers who grow your food
- the job that gives you the income to pay for your groceries
- the vehicle you have to get to the grocery store
- the fact that most of us have an abundance of food options at our fingertips every time we walk into a grocery store

The Lord gives us so many gifts that we take for granted.

At the peak of the toilet-paper shortages and the pandemic-induced panic buying in 2020, I admit that I started to worry about whether we would be able to get our staple food items. I'm not talking about a preferred toilet-paper brand. We had some specific items our family needed.

But then I realized something. If our usual store didn't have what I needed, there were dozens of other stores I could check within a twenty-mile radius of our home. And if I couldn't find what I needed at any of those, I could buy it online or drive however far I needed to get it. What a blessing!

To be honest, there have been times when I've looked at the overflowing bags of groceries sitting on our kitchen floor, waiting to be put away, and I've been moved to tears. And when I'm putting things away and the fridge and the cabinets are stuffed, I can't complain; I can only be thankful. What a blessing and what a responsibility to exercise gratitude and charity!

St. Isidore the Farmer and Bl. Maria Torribia were a married couple who embodied gratitude and charity perfectly. During a long day in the fields, Isidore would often give away most of his packed lunch, and later, he would bring home hungry workers who had nothing to eat. Maria, knowing her husband was prone to doing this, would make extra soup to share. On at least one occasion, she was sure they were going to run out. Tradition holds that Isidore assured her there was plenty, and miraculously, there was enough soup to ladle out to the guests.

We encourage families to pray for the intercession of St. Isidore and Bl. Maria for a couple of reasons. First, because St. Isidore is the patron of farmers, who grow everything we have to eat.

We also look at them as examples of heroic gratitude and charity, always willing to share what they had with others. Who knows how many souls they fed—and how many we can feed as well!

The next time you're unpacking your groceries, say this prayer of thanksgiving for all that you have and for the people who labored to bring your food from field to table.

Let us pray:

O God, through the example of St. Isidore the Farmer and Bl. Maria Torribia, You give us a beautiful example of a married couple's generosity and Christian charity. We thank You for the farmers who grew our food; for the truckers who transported it to the stores; for the grocers who stocked the shelves; and for the means by which we can afford this food. We thank You for our full fridge and full pantry. We ask that You bestow on us a greater sense of charity, that we, like Isidore and Maria, might be the best stewards of these gifts, always ready to share them with others. Amen.

Passing Prayer

O God, thank You for our full refrigerator and pantry. Inspire us to be more generous with what we have so that we may be ready to give and to help those who go without. Amen.

St. Fiacre and a Prayer for Success in the Garden

600–670 • FEAST DAY: AUGUST 30 • PATRON OF GARDENERS, FLORISTS, AND POTTERS

As for what was sown on good soil, this is he who hears the word and understands it; he indeed bears fruit, and yields, in one case a hundredfold, in another sixty, and in another thirty.

—Matthew 13:23

I think Dave is the most successful novice gardener I've ever seen. If there's anyone I know who has a natural gift for gardening, it's Dave.

He recently discovered that he finds great joy in working the land, researching plant needs, and cultivating a dramatic visual of his love for me. He has given me several rose and peony bushes, countless daffodils, gigantic allium, vibrant hyacinth, stunning lilac, fragrant Russian sage, and a sea of jumbo tulips in the spring. We're talking about *hundreds* of gigantic pink tulips, which we are able to cut and share with all our neighbors!

And you should hear his plans for the fruit and vegetable garden in the backyard! Dave is amazing! Well, enough gushing about my husband.

St. Fiacre was an Irish monk and is included here for his intercession for gardening success, not out of superstition, but out of an admiration for his love of creation—and not only for his love of creation but for his recognition of how God shows His love for us through creation.

We're not asking for St. Fiacre's help in producing an enviable garden for the sake of having an enviable garden; rather, we are asking not only for a successful yield but also for an awareness of God's love for us. Fiacre was known for growing vegetables and herbs, which he used as remedies for the sick. Tradition tells us that he once asked his local bishop for more land to grow food and herbs. The bishop told Fiacre he could have as much land as he could clear in a day. Using the point of his staff, he cleared such an impressive amount of acreage that the bishop declared the feat an act of God, a miracle.

Next time you're out in your garden, whether it be to pull weeds, prune bushes, lay mulch, or simply to enjoy the beauty, ask for the intercession of St. Fiacre, that you might offer up your labor and the fruits of your labor for the glory of God and for holiness for your family.

Let us pray:

St. Fiacre, skilled gardener and miraculous healer, thank you for your example of holiness as you used your vocation to serve the Lord. I ask that you watch over me as I work in my garden, not only for a successful yield but also that I might be ever aware of God's love for me. Like you, may I use my time to bring the love of God to my neighbor through my gardening. Amen.

Passing Prayer

St. Fiacre, skilled gardener and miraculous healer, watch over me as I work in my garden. Amen.

St. Gertrude the Great, a Prayer for the Holy Souls in Purgatory, and a Prayer for Deceased Family Members

1256–1302 • FEAST DAY: NOVEMBER 16 • PATRON OF TRAVELERS, RECENTLY DECEASED, AND THE WEST INDIES

Every time we look at the Blessed Sacrament, our place in heaven is raised forever.[65]

—St. Gertrude the Great

St. Gertrude is well deserving of her title "the Great." As of this writing, she's one of only a handful of saints who are called "the Great" (Pope St. Gregory the Great, Pope St. Leo the Great, Pope St. Nicholas the Great, St. Albert the Great, and some people refer to Pope St. John Paul II as "the Great") and is the only female saint to be named as such.

She's known for her intellect, her mysticism, and her commitment to living the Rule of St. Benedict in her monastery. She spent

[65] "Quotes on the Most Blessed Sacrament," Real Presence Association, http://www.therealpresence.org/eucharst/tes/quotes14.html.

years acquiring knowledge and becoming learned in poetry and culture, but she realized she was missing out on what mattered most in life.

After Jesus appeared to her in a dream, Gertrude vowed to spend her life growing in knowledge of theology and seeking deeper union with God. She began to see how her faults offended God and how His mercy was ever greater. This prepared her for suffering at the end of her life, which she accepted as God's gift of love and goodness.

Today, she's best known for praying for the poor souls in Purgatory and for a specific prayer attributed to her. It is said that, when it is prayed piously, Our Lord will release one thousand souls from Purgatory.[66] So let's get praying!

Let us pray:

St. Gertrude's Prayer for the Release of One Thousand Souls from Purgatory:

> Eternal Father, I offer Thee the Most Precious Blood of Thy Divine Son, Jesus, in union with the Masses said throughout the world today, for all the holy souls in Purgatory, for sinners everywhere, for sinners in the universal Church, those in my own home and within my family. Amen.

We also have a brief passing prayer for deceased loved ones. Please do not forget to pray for them. We like to think that our grandmas and grandpas are in Heaven, but we never know. Even

[66] Note: St. Gertrude's prayer does not convey an indulgence and does not have the conditions of an indulgence attached. Because it is said that Our Lord gave her this prayer, the devout recitation alone is sufficient.

if they are already in Heaven, our prayers for them will gain greater glory for them.

Passing Prayer

Eternal rest grant unto (*Name*), O Lord, and let perpetual light shine upon him/her. May he/she rest in peace. Amen.

St. Josephine Bakhita and a Prayer for the Grace to Forgive

1869–1947 • FEAST DAY: FEBRUARY 8 • PATRON OF SUDAN AND HUMAN-TRAFFICKING SURVIVORS

If I were to meet the slave traders who kidnapped me and even those who tortured me, I would kneel and kiss their hands, for if that did not happen, I would not be a Christian and Religious today.[67]

—St. Josephine Bakhita

If you've ever been hurt by someone before, you know how hard it can be to forgive. If you're struggling to ask for the grace to forgive someone, look to St. Josephine Bakhita.

Josephine was born into a happy, loving home in Darfur, Sudan. As a young child, she was kidnapped and sold into slavery several times. She was forced to convert to Islam, experienced various forms of torture, including branding, beating, and cutting, and suffered the tremendous emotional trauma of being taken from her family.

Through God's grace, because He had a great plan for her life, she was exposed to the Catholic Faith, chose to be baptized,

[67] Quoted in "St. Josephine Bakhita," Catholic News Agency, https://www.catholicnewsagency.com/saint/st-josephine-bakhita-680.

won her freedom, and entered religious life in Italy. Despite the horrible things that had happened to her, Bakhita spent the rest of her life serving God cheerfully and being a radiant witness to others. She had found not only freedom from physical slavery but spiritual freedom in Christ.

At one point, a student asked Bakhita what she would do if she encountered her captors again, and she replied, "If I were to meet the slave traders who kidnapped me and even those who tortured me, I would kneel and kiss their hands, for if that did not happen, I would not be a Christian and Religious today."

Instead of being trapped in the slavery of resentment when others hurt us, we must ask for the grace to forgive. It's difficult, I know. That's why we need God's grace.

Let us pray:

Lord, I'm plagued by the hurt I've experienced in my life, and I'm finding it hard to want to forgive. I ask that, through the intercession of St. Josephine Bakhita, I might receive the graces necessary to forgive those who have hurt me. St. Josephine Bakhita, model of forgiveness, obtain for me the grace to forgive. Amen.

Passing Prayer

St. Josephine Bakhita, model of forgiveness, help me to pray for the grace to forgive. Amen.

St. John Vianney and a Prayer for Your Parish Priest

1786–1859 • FEAST DAY: AUGUST 4 •
PATRON OF PARISH PRIESTS

The priesthood is the love of the Heart of Jesus.
When you see a priest,
think of Our Lord Jesus Christ.[68]

—St. John Vianney

Did you know that the heart of St. John Vianney is incorrupt? That's right. The heart of the patron saint of parish priests, who lived centuries ago, has not decomposed.

This is the heart that belonged to a little boy who admired the bravery of priests and nuns in the midst of the French Reign of Terror; Catholics, especially clergy, faced extreme persecution and death during the French Revolution and had to practice their Faith in secret.

This is the heart that beat with joy when he received First Holy Communion in a neighbor's kitchen while the celebrating priest offered Mass on the run.

[68] Quoted in Karna Swanson, "Curé d'Ars: Model Priest," Zenit, June 19, 2009, posted on EWTN, https://www.ewtn.com/catholicism/library/cur-dars-model-priest-9219.

This is the heart of a young man who struggled to learn Latin and to keep up with his education yet persevered out of a firm desire to become a priest.

This is the heart of the priest who arrived at the town of Ars, France, to minister to a people who did not know their Catholic Faith. He preached the truth in love to them, shepherding the lost sheep and patiently catechizing them.

This is the heart of the priest who would hear confessions for up to eighteen hours a day and would bring the sacraments to souls entrusted to him.

Your parish priest has a heart too, and it beats in service for you. He has renounced many of the pleasures of the world and has taken up an enormous cross for you. As St. John Vianney says,

> The priest is not a priest for himself; he does not give himself absolution; he does not administer the Sacraments to himself; he is not for himself; he is for you.[69]

Pray for your parish priest every single day, without exception. Be kind to him. Invite him over for dinner. Show him how grateful you are for his vocation. I wonder how many priests like St. John Vianney there would be if more people prayed for their pastors.

Let us pray:

Lord, I praise You for the gift of our priest, (*Name*). Watch over him and grant him the grace to be always faithful to You. May he love and serve our parish with a heart like St. John Vianney's, burning with love of You and love of his flock. Amen.

[69] St. Jean-Marie Baptiste Vianney, *The Little Catechism of the Curé d'Ars* (Rockford, IL: TAN Books, 1994), chap. 9.

Passing Prayer

Lord, I praise You for the gift of our priest, (*Name*). Watch over him and grant him the grace to be always faithful to You. Amen.

St. Gerard Majella and a Prayer of the Expectant Mother

1726–1755 • FEAST DAY: OCTOBER 16 • PATRON OF PREGNANT WOMEN, UNBORN CHILDREN, AND MOTHERHOOD

Who except God can give you peace? Has the world ever been able to satisfy the heart?[70]

—St. Gerard Majella

"Who except God can give you peace?" What a reminder for a pregnant woman, who has so many worries throughout her nine months of being with child:

- Will my baby be healthy?
- Why am I feeling cramping?
- Was that a kick?
- When will this morning sickness end?
- What if I go into labor early?
- Will we make it to the hospital in time?

[70] Quoted in Francis W. Johnston, *Voices of the Saints: Counsels from the Saints to Bring Comfort and Guidance in Daily Living* (Charlotte, NC: TAN Books, 2003), chap. 2.

- What if my milk doesn't come in?
- Will I develop postpartum depression?
- What if I don't feel a bond with my child?
- How will I function without sleep?

I know many of these worries because I have experienced them. When pregnant with our second child, our son, I started hemorrhaging at around fifteen weeks. I remember calling my friend, who dropped everything to come to our apartment to watch our daughter while I rushed to the hospital. Dave was in clinicals and couldn't leave. I was sobbing the whole way to the doctor and during the ultrasound. My doctor was not there that day, so another doctor saw me and reported, "I'm not going to promise you everything will be okay when it very well might not be."

"*What?*" I thought.

For the rest of the pregnancy, I was plagued by the worry that something could go wrong with our baby at any point. But I did find consolation in knowing I had the intercession of the saints—our usual saints, St. Joseph, St. Gianna, St. Gerard (the patron of unborn babies and expectant mothers), plus St. Anthony (we promised to name our son Anthony if St. Anthony protected him). A dear priest friend of ours happened to obtain a relic of St. Gerard, and we had it with us when I delivered our little Anthony, who was born healthy and absolutely perfect.

It might seem odd that a young Redemptorist brother, who was only twenty-nine at the time of his death, is invoked as a patron of pregnant women. Shortly before his death, he was visiting a family, and upon leaving, he dropped his handkerchief. When one of the daughters tried to return it to him, he told her to keep it, as it would be useful to her one day. Years down the road, when that same young woman was pregnant, she experienced complications during labor. She recalled the words of St. Gerard and sent for the handkerchief. Immediately upon receiving the handkerchief, her pain ceased and she delivered a healthy baby. See how quickly this saint is willing to come to your assistance when you ask for his intercession!

Let us pray:

St. Gerard, patron of unborn children and expectant mothers, I come to you with these concerns about my pregnancy (*state your concerns*). I ask that, through your intercession, I might find consolation and peace and place my trust and hope in the Lord. Pray for my unborn baby and me, for a safe and healthy delivery. Amen.

Passing Prayer

St. Gerard, patron of unborn children and expectant mothers, pray for my unborn baby and me. Amen.

St. Thomas Aquinas and a Prayer for Chastity for the Entire Family

1225–1274 • FEAST DAY: JANUARY 28 • PATRON OF STUDENTS, UNIVERSITIES, THEOLOGIANS, CHASTITY, AND MORE

In the realm of evil thoughts none induces
to sin as much as do thoughts that
concern the pleasure of the flesh.[71]

—St. Thomas Aquinas

St. Thomas Aquinas is one of the greatest theologians of all time. He wrote the *Summa theologica*, a compilation of all the Church's teachings that is thousands of pages long. He composed proofs for the existence of God. He highlighted the harmony of faith and reason, showing how nothing the Catholic Church teaches contradicts logic or reason.

So why is he invoked by those pursuing chastity? Well, before St. Thomas Aquinas was born, it is said that a hermit told his mother that her son would be so learned and so extraordinary in sanctity that none would be found equal to him.

[71] Quoted in Joseph M. Esper, *More Saintly Solutions to Life's Common Problems* (Manchester, NH: Sophia Institute Press, 2006), 181.

His family, of nobility, sent him off to school, where he proved to be an exceptional student. His heart, however, longed for the religious life, and he joined the Dominicans. Outraged at the thought of Thomas becoming a poor preacher, his family kidnapped him, locked him in their castle tower, and even sent a woman to seduce him, convinced he'd be tempted enough to abandon religious life. But he angrily drove the woman out with a poker from the fireplace, branded the sign of the cross on the door, and fell to the ground, praying for purity and chastity. Thomas reportedly entered a great sleep and received a vision of two angels, who girded him with a cord of chastity, never to be overpowered.

Even today, the Angelic Warfare Confraternity exists to pray for chastity and purity for men and women throughout the world. We are members of this confraternity and pray daily for chastity and purity for our family.

You can do the same. In a world that glorifies disordered sexual behavior, promiscuity, and sins of the flesh, there is a desperate need for us parents to pray for protection for our entire family (yes, even married couples must pray for chastity and purity).

Let us pray:

O Jesus, through the intercession of St. Thomas Aquinas, I pray for chastity and purity for my family. Guard our eyes, our minds, and our hearts from the stain of sin, and grant that we might surrender ourselves to Your will and Your will alone. Amen.

Passing Prayer

O Jesus, through the intercession of St. Thomas Aquinas, I pray for chastity and purity for my family. Amen.

St. Martin de Porres and a Prayer for the Completion of Housework

1579–1639 • FEAST DAY: NOVEMBER 3 • PATRON OF INNKEEPERS, RACE RELATIONS, BIRACIAL PEOPLE, PEOPLE OF COLOR, AND MORE

Everything, even sweeping, scraping vegetables, weeding a garden, and waiting on the sick could be a prayer, if it were offered to God.[72]

—Said of St. Martin de Porres

As parents with young children, we always have dishes to wash, loads of laundry to do, and floors to sweep and mop. In my house, crumbs seem to grow up from the floorboards; even after I sweep, there is always something on the floor! We have shelves to dust, decluttering to do, and toys to put away. No wonder we're tired parents! Cleaning up after kids is a full-time job!

When I was growing up, I despised doing chores. Chores were always treated as a punishment instead of an opportunity to have a tidy, peaceful home. That negative attitude carried into adulthood, and for a long time, I still didn't enjoy or appreciate cleaning.

[72] Mary Fabyan Windeatt, *Saint Martin de Porres: The Story of the Little Doctor of Lima, Peru* (Rockford, IL: TAN Books, 1979), chap. 6.

The real transformation in doing chores came when I realized that every part of house cleaning can be offered as a prayer.

I can delight in folding laundry because my family has clothes to wear. I can contemplate the precious memories made in those clothes, chuckle at the kids' preferences for certain articles, praise God for my husband's job while folding his work uniforms, and so on.

I can delight in doing dishes because my family has more than enough to eat. Our children have their colorful cups and plates, and I think about the fun we have making silly, kid-friendly meals they swoon over. I feel at peace when the kitchen is back in order, and I thank God that we have an endless supply of hot water.

I know this sounds bizarre, but I can delight in picking up the toys when I think about how much the kids enjoy playing together, when I think about their little imaginations at work, and when they start to clean up alongside me because they want to be helpers.

St. Martin de Porres knew this secret to enjoying housework, and he learned to do even the most menial tasks out of love. As a lay Dominican in Peru, he was responsible for cleaning, sweeping, kitchen duties, laundry, and caring for the sick. Most of his life was spent working and praying. He joyfully completed these tasks and saw the great graces that came from humbly serving his fellow Dominican brothers as well as the poor and the sick in their care.

And the Lord used Martin, who found prayerfulness in the ordinary, to bring about extraordinary, miraculous cures both during and after his life.

When it comes to being tired parents, we have two choices: we can grumble about chores and let resentment fester, or we can embrace the small cross of housework and offer the completion of tasks for the ones we love or for other intentions. I can assure you that it makes a huge difference to choose the latter!

Sometimes the chores are still overwhelming, and I'm still not fond of constantly cleaning, but when I can offer up my duties for the salvation of my family, I am reminded of the gift of my vocation and the opportunities to praise God in my state of life.

Let us pray:

St. Martin de Porres, the housework never really ends, does it? Help me find joy and satisfaction in the work I do to keep up my home. As I sweep the floors, help me to give thanks for the feet that walk along them. As I wash the dishes, help me to give thanks for the mouths that eat from them. As I dust the shelves, help me to give thanks for the faces in the photos that grace them. As I fold the clothes, help me to give thanks for the people who wear them. As I pick up the toys, help me to give thanks for my children, who play with them. Amen.

Passing Prayer

St. Martin de Porres, help me find joy in my housework. Amen.

St. Teresa of Ávila and a Prayer for Perseverance amid Persecution

1515–1582 • FEAST DAY: OCTOBER 15 • PATRON OF PEOPLE RIDICULED FOR THEIR PIETY, HEADACHE AND MIGRAINE SUFFERERS, AND MORE

It takes great humility to find oneself unjustly condemned and be silent, and to do this is to imitate the Lord Who set us free from all our sins.... The truly humble person will have a genuine desire to be thought little of, and persecuted, and condemned unjustly, even in serious matters.[73]

—St. Teresa of Ávila

St. Teresa of Ávila is one of only four female Doctors of the Church. She didn't start out as a saint, but not many do. She grew up with parents in a difficult marriage. Her father was extremely strict, and Teresa often became distracted by the ways of the world. She entered religious life only because it was less strict than her father's rules. Once secure in her vocation, however, she discovered that the convent was in trouble. The nuns themselves were too worldly, focusing on money, jewelry, and social status. They held parties at

[73] *The Way of Perfection*, trans. and ed. E. Allison Peers (New York: Image, 1964), chap. 15.

the convent, often with male guests. And the nuns made ostentatious displays of "piety," flailing their arms and inducing hysteria.

I could go on and on about her story, conversion, and reform of the Church, but that would be a book in and of itself, with a sequel about what parents can learn from her spirituality.

Here's what is important to know as it relates to perseverance amid persecution:

When St. Teresa of Ávila became convinced that she needed to reform her order, it was a struggle, and she faced bitter persecution for it. She wanted the Carmelites to go back to basics with their spirituality, living lives of contemplation, poverty, and prayer. She was trying to do the right thing out of love for Christ and His Church, but she faced public denouncement, condemnation, and humiliation for it. She was defamed by the papal nuncio and accused of being a devil worshipper. Even her closest friends turned on her. Still, she kept the faith.

When I look at Teresa of Ávila's life, and how she was willing to turn from the world to seek God in all things, I'm reminded that nothing else matters if I don't love God above everything. When I see how she stood firm in defense of the Faith and was unwavering in her commitment to prayer, I'm inspired to take my Faith more seriously. And when I see how patiently and humbly she endured unjust persecution, I'm given the strength to face persecution in my own life.

Let us pray:

St. Teresa of Ávila, you bravely endured persecution out of love for truth. Help me in my trials today, as I, too, face ridicule for trying to live my Faith. Amen.

Passing Prayer

St. Teresa of Ávila, help me in my trials today. Amen.

St. Veronica and a Prayer While Assisting Someone Carrying a Cross

FIRST CENTURY AD • FEAST DAY: JULY 12 • PATRON OF PHOTOGRAPHERS, FILM CREATORS, AND LAUNDRY WORKERS

Truly, I say to you, as you did it to one of the least of these my brethren, you did it to me.

—Matthew 25:40

In Christianity, we refer to our sufferings as "crosses." We all have crosses to bear, some heavier than others.

But how often do we consider the need to help others carry their crosses? There was Simon of Cyrene, who physically carried the Cross for Jesus during His journey to Calvary. And there was Veronica, who emerged from the crowd to offer a simple gesture of kindness toward Jesus, Whose face was dripping with sweat and blood. Unfazed by the soldiers and the screaming and chaos around her, she reached out to wipe Jesus' face with her veil. The gesture seemed insignificant to the rest of the world, but Jesus rewarded her greatly, imprinting His Holy Face on her veil.

Do we attempt to assist others with their crosses? Like Veronica, we can't take away the crosses. We might not even be able to help carry them, as did Simon of Cyrene. But we can show love and mercy. We can be a listening ear. We can pray and make sacrifices for those who are suffering. And in a world that is suffering so much, none of us has an excuse to slip back into the crowd unnoticed. We all should be like Veronica, ready and willing to offer comfort and relief.

Let us pray:

Jesus, You know well the pain of human suffering, because You experienced it in Your bitter Passion. Veronica, doing all she could, offered her veil to bring You comfort. Grant me the grace and the fortitude to extend that same selflessness to my neighbors as they carry their crosses. I offer my small acts of charity for love of You. Imprint your Face on my heart as I strive to ease the burdens of my neighbors. Amen.

Passing Prayer

Jesus, I offer my small acts of charity for love of You. Amen.

St. Dymphna and a Prayer for a Family Enduring Mental Illness

SEVENTH CENTURY • FEAST DAY: MAY 15 • PATRON OF RUNAWAYS, ABUSE VICTIMS, AND THOSE SUFFERING FROM MENTAL ILLNESS

Peace I leave with you; my peace I give to you; not as the world gives do I give to you. Let not your hearts be troubled, neither let them be afraid.

—John 14:27

When people suffer from mental illness, their family and friends suffer alongside them. This is evident in the life of St. Dymphna, a seventh-century saint from Ireland.

Dymphna was born to a pagan king and a Christian mother. She was raised Christian. At an early age, Dymphna consecrated herself to God as a virgin. After her mother's death, Dymphna's father experienced a sharp decline in his mental health. He was advised to take a second wife but was unable to find any woman as beautiful and lovely as his wife; that is, until he considered his own daughter. Dymphna refused and fled to Belgium with her confessor and his companions. Her deranged father hunted her down, however, and, after she again refused to be his wife, he killed both Dymphna and her confessor. For these reasons, St. Dymphna is invoked as the patron saint of those who suffer from mental illness and sexual abuse, since she was the victim of an attempted sexual assault.

I don't want to give the impression that Catholics try to *pray away* mental illness. Rather, when we consider the life of Our Lord and the suffering He faced, and when we see the suffering the saints endured, we're able to find comfort and strength.

The *Catechism of the Catholic Church* details how suffering unites us with Christ, gives us a share in His redemption of mankind, and can be offered for the salvation of souls (see CCC 1499–1532).

Mental illness and traumas are endured by the entire family, so when family members suffer in this way, we must carry that cross together. That means we all need to pray for the grace to face the suffering bravely, to work for life-giving solutions, and to uphold the dignity of our loved ones.

Let us pray:

Lord, be with us as our family endures the pain of (*mental illness, abuse, etc.*). This is a heavy cross, and we cannot bear it alone. Through the intercession of St. Dymphna, virgin and martyr, we pray for the grace to remain united as a family of faith, and we pray that this suffering will be for Your glory. Amen.

Passing Prayer

St. Dymphna, pray for us as we carry this cross together. Amen.

St. Peregrine and a Prayer for an Ill Family Member

1265–1345 • FEAST DAY: MAY 1 • PATRON OF THOSE SUFFERING FROM CANCER, FOOT AILMENTS, AND OTHER DISEASES

Naked I came from my mother's womb, and naked shall I return; the Lord *giveth, and the* Lord *taketh away. Blessed be the name of the* Lord.

—Job 1:21

Families of those suffering from cancer will quickly turn to St. Peregrine Laziosi, the patron of those with cancer, foot ailments, and other diseases.

Peregrine lived in a city that had so greatly lost its faith that the pope placed the city under interdict as an act of mercy to prompt the people's conversion. Peregrine himself joined a gang of rebels who beat up the papal ambassador sent to reconcile the city (later known as St. Philip Benizi). But Peregrine immediately regretted attacking the priest, begged for forgiveness, and from that moment on, became fervent in his Faith.

He was ordained a priest and founded a monastery in his hometown. Ironically, the same town he lived in while rebelling against the Faith became the town that later called him the "Angel of Good Counsel" for his preaching and his serving the poor. He spent decades in the service of God and making reparation for his sins.

At the age of sixty, he developed a cancerous growth on his foot that required medical attention. The night before his scheduled amputation, he prayed for hours and hours. He then fell asleep and dreamed that the Lord touched him and healed his foot. When he awoke, his foot was indeed healed.

After that, his fellow townsmen regularly came to him for healing of their diseases, some reportedly being cured when he whispered the Name of Jesus in their ears.

Centuries later, people still turn to St. Peregrine, asking for healing from cancer and other diseases. Though we cannot guarantee a miraculous healing in every case, we nevertheless continue asking for the help of this great saint, who shows us that God heals us in many ways. Along with praying for physical healing, we should remember to pray for an increase in strength, courage, and all the spiritual graces we need to carry the heavy cross of cancer and other diseases.

Let us pray:

O Lord, through the intercession of St. Peregrine, we pray for healing for (*Name*), who suffers from (*state the illness*). In your mercy, hear our prayer. Heal us of our own physical and spiritual illnesses. We trust in Your goodness and pray for the grace to be ever more attuned to Your loving will. Amen.

Passing Prayer

O Lord, through the intercession of St. Peregrine, heal us of our physical and spiritual illnesses. Amen.

Sts. Louis and Zélie Martin and a Prayer for Homemakers and Work-from-Home Parents

1823–1894; 1831–1877 • FEAST DAY: JULY 12 • PATRONS OF MARRIED COUPLES; INVOKED AS PATRON OF BUSINESSWOMEN AND WORK-FROM-HOME PARENTS

It is necessary for the heroic to become everyday and for the everyday to become heroic.[74]

—Said in reference to St. Zélie Martin

Sts. Louis and Zélie, parents of St. Thérèse of Lisieux, were the first married couple to be canonized together. They are a Catholic *power couple* for their faithfulness to God throughout their lives, even in the face of tragedy and tremendous suffering.

Both Louis and Zélie felt called to religious life, but God had different plans. Louis became a watchmaker, and Zélie became a lacemaker. For a while after they were married, they lived as celibates, until a priest convinced them to be open to life. They had

[74] Quoted in a homily of Cardinal José Saraiva Martins, July 2008, in "The Spirituality of Louis & Zélie," Sanctuary of Lisieux, https://www.therese-de-lisieux.catholique.fr/en/lhistoire/la-spiritualite-de-louis-et-zelie/.

nine children, four of whom died in infancy, and five of whom entered religious life.

The Martins are often invoked for their intercession by homemakers, businesswomen, and work-from-home parents, and for good reason. Somehow, while raising so many children, Zélie ran a successful business—so successful that Louis was able to sell his watchmaking business to go all-in with her.

That doesn't mean that Zélie wasn't completely exhausted. Quite the contrary! She had several women working for her as her business flourished, and she regularly woke at 5:00 a.m. and worked until 11:00 p.m. In her letters to Louis (who traveled to manage wholesale lace contracts), she is candid about her struggles with raising the children, keeping up with the business, and managing the household duties. And then, on top of everything else, she got breast cancer.

Yet she did it. The Martins bravely bore their crosses with love, fully aware of their mission to raise their children for Heaven. They truly are worthy of the title of "Saints."

Based on their life circumstances, Sts. Louis and Zélie can be invoked for a number of other reasons:

- For married couples and those discerning marriage
- For women in supervisory roles
- For parents suffering child loss
- For parents raising multiple daughters
- For couples discerning family size
- For young widowers
- For parents who struggle to find reliable childcare

- For parents of strong-willed children
- For women who fight injustices
- For breast-cancer sufferers

Whatever suffering the Lord permits for your good, ask the Martins for their intercession. If anyone modeled good, tired Catholic parenting well, it's Sts. Louis and Zélie.

Let us pray:

Sts. Louis and Zélie, I look to you for assistance with (*state your need*). Since you successfully raised five daughters who entered religious life, and since you modeled so beautifully the abandonment and trust required for Christian holiness, I ask with confidence for your heavenly friendship as I attempt to do the same in my life. Amen.

Passing Prayer

Sts. Louis and Zélie, I ask for your heavenly friendship today. Amen.

St. Lawrence and a Prayer When Everything Is Going Up in Flames

AD 225–258 • FEAST DAY: AUGUST 10 • PATRON OF COOKS, DEACONS, COMEDIANS, AND THE POOR

Turn me over; I'm done on this side!

—St. Lawrence

I guess we should offer a disclaimer at the start of this reflection that we absolutely do not intend any irreverence toward the saints, especially those who were brutally martyred in defense of the Faith. But the story of St. Lawrence, deacon and martyr, lends itself to allowing a touch of humor.

Lawrence was an archdeacon (head deacon) in the third century, when Christians faced relentless persecution in the Roman Empire. Lawrence was responsible for managing the Church's finances, giving alms to the poor, and ensuring the care of widows and orphans.

The emperor Valerian had ordered the death of all clergy, deacons included. Just days before Lawrence's death, Pope St. Sixtus II and Lawrence's six fellow deacons were beheaded.

As the sole remaining deacon and fully aware that he was in danger of martyrdom, Lawrence gave away all the money and treasures he could get his hands on, so that the empire would gain as little as possible.

Hearing about this stunt, a Roman official demanded that Lawrence hand over all the treasures of the Church. According to tradition, Lawrence requested three days to set everything in order and take inventory.

During those three days, he rounded up the widows, orphans, lepers, the poor, the blind, and the lame and presented them to the official, saying, "Here they are, the treasures of the Church!" Enraged, the official ordered Lawrence to be subject to a slow death by roasting on a gridiron. His last words were reportedly some variation of "Turn me over; I'm done on this side!"

There are plenty of things in life we can control, but so many more that we can't. When everything around us is going up in flames, and when there's nothing we can do about it, perhaps the best way to deal with the situation is with a bit of humor and a lot of surrender.

St. Lawrence knew he was going to die. Instead of cowering in fear, he boldly faced death with the cheerful disposition that has baffled the Church's persecutors for millennia. In Philippians 4, St. Paul exhorts us to "rejoice in the Lord always" and to "have no anxiety about anything," and if we do, he tells us, "the peace, which passes all understanding, will keep [our] hearts and [our] minds in Christ Jesus" (Phil. 4:4, 6).

Let us pray:

St. Lawrence, you knew how to make the best of the worst situation. Please be with me as everything is going up in flames in my life. Help me approach this with a light heart, a sound mind, and a bit of humor. Remind me that the peace I seek can be found only when I surrender my will fully to Jesus Christ, our Savior. Amen.

Passing Prayer

St. Lawrence, be with me as everything is going up in flames. Amen.

Ven. Archbishop Fulton J. Sheen and a Prayer in Thanksgiving for Coffee

1895–1979 • DATE OF DEATH: DECEMBER 9 • PATRON OF MEDIA AND EVANGELIZATION

The average American is physically, biologically, physiologically and neurologically unable to do anything worthwhile before he has a cup of coffee! And that goes for prayer too.... Let them have coffee before meditation.[75]

—Ven. Archbishop Fulton J. Sheen

One year, I told Dave I wanted to give up coffee for Lent. He roped in a priest friend of ours, who forbade me to give up coffee. Both my husband and our priest warned that I would not be able to fulfill my duties as a wife, mother, and full-time employee if I gave up coffee for forty days. Even worse, it might cause me to sin! Honestly, I don't even drink much coffee—maybe sixteen ounces a day.

[75] Quoted in Celeste Behe, "Let Them Drink Coffee," *National Catholic Register*, January 25, 2022, https://www.ncregister.com/blog/let-them-drink-coffee.

This year, I took a different approach. Instead of giving up coffee entirely, I decided to drink bitter coffee every morning. For someone who finds great enjoyment in a hot cup of sweet, vanilla-caramel-flavored coffee straight from the French press, this was a bit brutal. Okay, it was more than *a bit* brutal.

With every sip of that hot, bitter bean water (aka black coffee), I reminded myself of the bitterness of my sins, my fallen nature, and my total dependence on God. Without His grace, His goodness, and His love, my life would be a bitter nothingness in the pits of Hell—far worse than forty days of black coffee. I might think I wouldn't last a day without coffee, but that isn't true at all. The truth is that I wouldn't last a day without *God*.

In his televised teaching series, Ven. Archbishop Fulton J. Sheen sought to remind viewers, Americans in particular, of our need for God. He was known for addressing the social issues of the day. He frequently pointed out that we have become so comfortable with the technology and luxuries of the world that we have forgotten the sweetness of God. Our souls are steeped in the bitterness of consumerism, godlessness, lawlessness, selfishness, and sin, but we don't even realize the goodness we are missing out on because we're hell-bent (literally!) on the instant gratification that the world offers.

But take heart. Drinking coffee is amoral. You can enjoy your coffee in the morning, prepared however you like. Just don't lose sight of your absolute dependence on God.

Let us pray:

Lord, I give You thanks for this cup of coffee. And though I feel I cannot do anything worthwhile without it, I know that I truly cannot do anything without You. Let this morning brew be a reminder to me that all I am and all I have is because of You. Please be patient with me today. I give my day to You, for Your glory. Amen.

Passing Prayer

Lord, I can't do anything without You. Use me for Your glory! Amen.

Bl. Carlo Acutis and a Prayer for Good Use of the Internet

1991–2006 • FEAST DAY: OCTOBER 12 • PATRON OF YOUTH AND COMPUTER PROGRAMMERS

I am happy to die because I have lived my life without wasting a minute on those things which do not please God.[76]

—Bl. Carlo Acutis

I look at the quote above by Bl. Carlo Acutis, and I feel my heart drop into my stomach. How much time have I wasted on things that do not please God? How much time have I wasted mindlessly browsing the Internet, scrolling through social media newsfeeds, checking out profiles of complete strangers, binging on nostalgic TV series, and going down the rabbit hole of random topics that truly are a waste of time and give no honor to God?

How tragic, truly. Are you lamenting it too?

In today's age, we need Bl. Carlo's life and witness so badly. He was not a saint from centuries ago. He was born in 1991! He grew up with the Internet. He was alive in the age of Myspace and AIM and Facebook. He played video games and owned a cell phone.

[76] "Introduction," Official Website of the Carlo Acutis Association and the Cause of Canonization of Blessed Carlo Acutis, http://www.carloacutis.com/en/association/presentazione.

Do you know how he used his time on the Internet? He used his skills as a so-called computer geek to create an online catalog of all the world's recorded Eucharistic miracles, which he started at age eleven and completed in 2005. That catalog is still accessible at CarloAcutis.com.

Even though he died of leukemia at the tender age of fifteen, he exhibited great spiritual maturity and possessed wisdom well beyond his years. Perhaps that was due to the significant time he spent at daily Mass and in Eucharistic Adoration. He called the Eucharist his "Highway to Heaven," and he definitely took the expressway!

Like Bl. Carlo Acutis, our entire family can strive to make good use of the Internet and all digital media.

Let us pray:

Lord, You gave us Bl. Carlo Acutis to model Christian perfection in today's digital world. We ask that, through his intercession, we might be good stewards of our time and use the Internet in a way that pleases You. Amen.

Passing Prayer

Bl. Carlo Acutis, help us to use the Internet in a way that pleases God. Amen.

Sts. Kizito and José Sánchez del Río and a Prayer for Courage for Children

1872–1886; 1913–1928 • FEAST DAY: JUNE 3; FEBRUARY 10 • PATRONS OF CHILDREN AND PERSECUTED CHRISTIANS

We will see each other in Heaven. Viva Cristo Rey![77]

—St. José Sanchez del Río

The protective parent in me doesn't want to think about the idea of our children being martyrs. But then I can't help but think about the glorious witness of the young martyrs our Church has produced—St. Maria Goretti, St. Agnes, St. Tarcisius, St. Philomena, St. Pancras, St. Lucy, St. Dymphna, Bl. Laura Vicuna, the Holy Innocents who died in Jesus' place under Herod's rule, and so many young martyrs—and these are all in addition to the non-martyred young saints of the Church!

At age fourteen, St. Kizito was the youngest of the Ugandan Martyrs killed by the king of Buganda. Kizito, along with St. Charles Lwanga and their companions, served as pages for the king, who was a pedophile. The head pages did their best to protect the

[77] Quoted in Fr. Kevin McKenzie, *Saint José: Boy Cristero Martyr* (San Francisco: Ignatius Press, 2019), 176.

young boys from the advances of the king, but the king eventually sentenced all of them to death.

On their way to execution, Kizito and the others joyfully sang together. Kizito's last reported words were, "Goodbye, my friends. We are on the right path." Those who witnessed the martyrs' deaths were so inspired that some chose to be baptized.

Known as "Joselito," St. José Sánchez del Río was a flagbearer for the Cristero movement in Mexico during the Cristero War. When his brothers joined the rebels, Joselito's mother tried to stop him from joining too, but he insisted that he wanted to give his life for Christ.

Joselito was captured by government troops, who pressured him to renounce his Catholic Faith. He refused. They forced him to watch the hanging of another Cristero, but it didn't break Joselito's resolve. He encouraged his comrade. Some of his last words were "We will see each other in Heaven. Viva Cristo Rey!"

Since they were unable to scare Joselito into apostasy, they cut off the bottoms of his feet and forced him on a death march, cutting him with a machete. He continued to pray the Rosary, prayed for his persecutors, and sang hymns of praise. He died just shy of his fifteenth birthday.

It is less likely that our children will end up being killed for their Faith and more likely that they will face intense persecution for their Faith. They will be pressured by their friends to commit sin and reject the Faith. They will be pressured by authorities to commit sin and reject the Faith. They will be pressured by the culture to commit sin and reject the Faith.

As parents, we must pray unceasingly for protection for our children. We must also pray for courage and steadfast faith in times of trouble. Our children will face hardships, and we will not always be there to protect them. Let us entrust our children to the

Blessed Mother and pray that they will be heroically virtuous like Kizito and Joselito! Know that we are praying for your children too.

While most of the prayers in this book are for parents to pray, this is a prayer to teach your children. Place this prayer where they can see it and pray it regularly.

Let us pray:

St. Kizito and St. José Sánchez del Río, you were both faithful to God, even when faced with death. Help me to be brave, even when it's hard. Help me to be faithful, even when I'm tempted. Help me to stay on the right path, even when others go down different paths. Be my friends and stay with me when I feel alone. Pray for me, so I can be happy in Heaven forever, like you. Amen.

Passing Prayer

St. Kizito and St. José Sánchez del Río, help me to be brave, even when it's hard. Amen.

St. John the Evangelist and a Prayer for Our Friends

DIED AD 100 • FEAST DAY: DECEMBER 27 • PATRON OF FRIENDSHIPS, LOYALTY, AUTHORS, AND LOVE

Beloved, let us love one another; for love is of God, and he who loves is born of God and knows God. . . . If we love one another, God abides in us and his love is perfected in us.

—1 John 4:7, 12

If Jesus had a best friend, I don't think it would be hard to guess who it would be—St. John, the Beloved Disciple. St. John himself tells us that he is referred to as "the disciple whom he loved" (John 19:26) and "the one whom Jesus loved" (John 20:2).

John is said to have been the youngest of the apostles. Alongside Peter and James, John was present for key moments in Jesus' ministry, such as the Transfiguration, the Agony in the Garden of Gethsemane, and the healing of Jairus's daughter. John sat closest to Jesus during the Last Supper and leaned on Him. He was the only apostle to stay with Jesus at the foot of the Cross, and Jesus entrusted His Mother to John, and John (and the Church) to His Mother. On hearing the news of the Resurrection on Easter Sunday, John ran to the empty tomb with Peter. The early Church Fathers say that John outlived the rest of the apostles and was the only one not to be martyred. He died of natural causes around AD 100.

By our worldly standards of friendship, John was a true friend, never abandoning Jesus, even when times were hard. I don't know about you, but during the happiest and toughest moments of life, Dave and I have found loyalty, companionship, consolation, and encouragement from both longtime friends and even newer friends.

We have been blessed with friendships:

- Our beloved friends celebrated with us in the joys of marriage and new babies.
- Our beloved friend dropped everything to be there when a pregnancy complication threatened us.
- Our beloved friends treat us with delicious baked goods and surprise mail, "just because."
- Our beloved friend never fails to check in on us day after day, knowing that we're busy with work and home renovations and parenthood.
- Our beloved friends are ready at a moment's notice to help with home renovation projects, even when they have their own projects to work on.
- Our beloved friend, despite having her hands full with her own family, is always ready to listen to us and to offer us a priceless, profound nugget of spiritual wisdom.
- Our beloved friends consoled us in moments of sorrow and suffering.
- Our beloved friend watched our kids for us while we were dealing with compounded crises at a chaotic time in our lives and never passed judgment on us or thought less of us when she witnessed us at rock bottom.

- Our beloved friends, who just so happen to be our biological siblings, have grown closer and closer to us over the years, sharing with us all the important moments of life.
- Our beloved "best priest friend" prepared us for marriage and promised, "I am in this with you for life."

Lord, what have we done to deserve these friends and blessings?

Think about your friends, and how they have been with you through thick and thin. Praise God for their lives and their love. Tell them how much you appreciate them! And strive to be a friend that a person would be blessed to have.

Let us pray:

Lord, we thank You with great awe and sincerity for the gift of our friends. Through the intercession of St. John the Apostle, Your own beloved friend, we ask that You might shower our friends with an abundance of blessings and with the consolation of Your presence, now and forever. Amen.

Passing Prayer

Lord, thank You for the gift of our friends. Shower them with an abundance of Your blessings, now and forever. Amen.

St. Polycarp and a Prayer for a Particular Need

AD 69–155 • FEAST DAY: FEBRUARY 23 • PATRON OF EARACHE SUFFERERS

Eighty and six years I have served Him,
and He has done me no wrong.[78]

—St. Polycarp

One day at work, I was lamenting to one of my superiors about the trouble I had finding a decent parking spot. (Just a warning: if you ask me, "How are you?" I'm going to tell you, even if it's not fabulous news.) Seeing how flustered I was, he suggested, "Next time, why don't you pray to St. Polycarp?"

"Saint Polycarp?" I responded, confused. "Shouldn't I pray to St. Anthony?"

"No, no, no, pray to Polycarp. Anthony is too busy up there. Polycarp isn't doing anything because no one asks him!"

Since then, when I need something, such as a parking spot, I ask St. Polycarp. And though that conversation was meant as a

[78] *Martyrdom of Polycarp*, chap. 9, from *Ante-Nicene Fathers*, vol. 1, ed. Alexander Roberts, James Donaldson, and A. Cleveland Coxe (Buffalo, NY: Christian Literature Publishing, 1885), revised and edited for New Advent by Kevin Knight, http://www.newadvent.org/fathers/0102.htm.

bit of innocent Catholic humor, I don't think this executive really expected that it would lead to my friendship with St. Polycarp, the early Church Father who was friends with the Beloved Apostle, St. John.

St. Polycarp is an excellent friend to enlist for specific needs throughout the day, but I like to call on him for the big stuff—the *fires* in my life. When he was being martyred, his executioners unsuccessfully tried to burn him at the stake. Though flames raged around him, he was not burned. He was then stabbed to death, and according to witness accounts, the blood that poured out of his body extinguished the fire beneath him.

When we pray for the intercession of the saints, it isn't always a quick fix. Praying to St. Polycarp for a parking spot at the front of the lot doesn't mean you're going to get it. However, praying for the intercession of the saints often leads us to change our outlook on a situation. Whereas we might have desired only one outcome, we can now suddenly be at peace with another. In the case of Polycarp, his brutal martyrdom was not the end of the road but his entrance into eternal Paradise. And as a faithful Christian, he knew it was a happy ending too.

Don't be afraid to go to the saints with your dire, urgent, or seemingly impossible needs. They know of God's goodness and can help us increase our faith and hope for a fruitful outcome!

Let us pray:

O Holy St. Polycarp, disciple of St. John the Apostle, you were faithful to the gospel your entire life, even in the face of a brutal death. Since you know so well the glories and goodness of God, and since you have a reputation for literally putting out fires, I ask you to assist me in my need (*state your need*). Help me also to grow in friendship with the saints, as you did, so that together we may all enjoy eternal Paradise with Christ Our Lord. Amen.

Passing Prayer

St. Polycarp, help me to put out the fires that ravage my life. Amen.

Prayer to All Our Friends, the Saints

ALL SAINTS' DAY: NOVEMBER 1

I want to spend my heaven in doing good on earth.[79]

—St. Thérèse of Lisieux

We have just reflected on the lives of more than thirty saints—amazing examples of everyday holiness and extraordinary, heroic virtue. They are men and women from different walks of life, united in their Catholic Faith and their love of Jesus in the Eucharist. They are saints who lived hard lives and faced challenges but persevered and won their heavenly reward.

We've not even begun to scratch the surface of the Church's saints throughout Her two-thousand-year history. Our hope is that these reflections will be helpful to you as you grow in friendship with the saints and that they will inspire you to seek friendship with more saints!

Here are some suggestions:

- Keep reading about the saints.
- Keep reading the writings of the saints.

[79] *St. Thérèse of Lisieux: Her Last Conversations*, trans. John Clarke, O.C.D. (Washington, DC: ICS Publications, 1977), 102.

- Keep asking for the help of the saints.
- Keep imitating their heroic virtue.
- Keep praying for your own sanctity and that you and your children will be numbered among the saints one day!

Let us pray.

Lord, we praise You for the gift of the saints. Grant us the grace to be receptive to their teachings, to seek their constant company, to ask their intercession, and to desire the grace to join them in Heaven with You forever. All ye holy men and women, pray for us! Amen.

Passing Prayer

All ye holy men and women of God, pray for us! Amen.

Family Prayer Journal

Lord God, I praise Your Holy Name. Let every beat of my heart be a note of love in the symphony of my life.

—Mother Angelica

Prayer of the heart is always a deep awareness of Who you're working for, Who you love, and Who loves you. That's why it's so important to pray constantly, continually, and not lose heart.

—Mother Angelica

The penance of this age is to be faithful to your duties in your state of life.

—Mother Angelica

God has our entire lives in the Palm of His Loving Hand. We can rest secure about our past, present, and future—for He loves us.

—Mother Angelica

Love is not a feeling. It is a decision. Jesus cannot command that you have a feeling. He can only command us to make a decision, and love is the greatest decision we will ever make.

—Mother Angelica

My Do/Drop System is to do it and drop it. When you live in the present moment, you do whatever must be done, then drop it and move on. You don't dwell on the past, or on your past accomplishments. That's all over. Do it and drop it.

—Mother Angelica

I must read the Gospels daily in order to absorb the Word into my soul. His Gospels are more than an example of what He accomplished; they give me the power to imitate that example and duplicate it in my own life.

—Mother Angelica

The only way to get to the Father's Heart is to admit who you are, to know your weaknesses and your faults.

—Mother Angelica

Let us ask Our Dear Lord for the graces we don't even know we need, the grace to endure the cross with serenity. I think that has to be one of the greatest gifts, and I'm sure not many ask for it.

—Mother Angelica

If we are so busy with the noise of the world, with the noise of events, with the noise of things around us, ourselves, our work, our friends, then even if it is extremely quiet, we can't hear anything. Our powers of concentration are so diverted that we cannot concentrate on God.

—Mother Angelica

The saint is the person who loves Jesus on a personal level—loves Him enough to want to be like Him in everyday life—loves Him enough to take on some of His lovable characteristics.

—Mother Angelica

Don't complain about the Church. You are the Church, and God has destined you to proclaim the Good News by example, by family life, by a holy single life, and by faithfulness.

—Mother Angelica

The real Christian lives in an atmosphere of prayer. For him, prayer is not a spiritual exercise that he performs on occasion; it is a way of life. There are times he says prayers, but those are times he asks for the things he needs. Most of his time is spent in preparing himself to live in God as God lives in Him.

—Mother Angelica

No matter what anybody says to you or about you, it is nothing compared with what you are in the Eyes of God.

—Mother Angelica

We must perseveringly train our senses and faculties to seek the hidden, silent presence of God in everything, that they may serve us well in our quest for holiness.

—Mother Angelica

It is very necessary, if you want to grow, that you read Scripture and other spiritual books of lives of saints, lives of holy men and women who had the courage and the strength to follow the gospel.

—Mother Angelica

We should never be discouraged or disheartened over our weaknesses. Jesus has given us His Spirit to help us to be more like Him. He has given us His shepherds to lead us back home. He has given us the grace we need to repent, change, and become holy.

—Mother Angelica

Sufferings that come from God purify your soul so that you can rise to higher heights. These sufferings may be intense, but they are the kind that make you grow.

—Mother Angelica

Though I conquered the world but never conquered myself, it would be nothing.

—Mother Angelica

You are God's beloved, the apple of His Eye. Each one of us, in our own way, with our own distinct personalities, graces, intellects, cultures, and everything else, must enhance the Church by having more faith and more love for Jesus every day.

—Mother Angelica

Our Family Litany of Saints

In the Name of the Father, and of the Son, and of the Holy Spirit. Amen.

V. Lord, have mercy.
R. Christ, have mercy.
V. Lord, have mercy on us. Christ, hear us.
R. Christ, graciously hear us.

V. God, the Father of Heaven.
R. Have mercy on us.
V. God the Son, Redeemer of the World,
R. Have mercy on us.
V. God the Holy Spirit,
R. Have mercy on us
V. Holy Trinity, one God,
R. Have mercy on us.

V. Holy Mary,
R. Pray for us
V. St. Joseph, . . .

V. All ye holy men and women of God,

R. Pray for us!

Heaven is your real home. This is our testing ground, that's all. We were created by God to be with Him. That's why it's so important to say yes to God in everything. Let Him guide you. Ask Him to give you all that you need to accept your way of life and to live it well.

—Mother Angelica

Appendix

Cut out the following prayers and post them where they will remind you to pray them regularly.

Morning Offering

O Jesus, through the Immaculate Heart of Mary, I offer You my prayers, works, joys, and sufferings of this day, for all the intentions of Thy Sacred Heart, in union with the Holy Sacrifice of the Mass throughout the world, in reparation for my sins, for the intentions of all my relatives and friends, and in particular for the intentions of the Holy Father. Amen.

Act of Spiritual Communion

My Jesus, I believe that You are present in the Most Holy Sacrament. I love You above all things, and I desire to receive You into my soul. Since I cannot at this moment receive You sacramentally, come at least spiritually into my heart. I embrace You as if You were already there and unite myself wholly to You. Never permit me to be separated from You. Amen.

Litany of Humility

V. Jesus, meek and humble of heart,
R. *Hear me.*

V. From the desire of being esteemed,
R. *Deliver me, Jesus.*
V. From the desire of being loved …
R. *Deliver me, Jesus.*
From the desire of being extolled …
From the desire of being honored …
From the desire of being praised …
From the desire of being preferred to others …
From the desire of being consulted …
From the desire of being approved …
From the fear of being humiliated …
From the fear of being despised …
From the fear of suffering rebukes …
From the fear of being calumniated …
From the fear of being forgotten …
From the fear of being ridiculed …
From the fear of being wronged …
From the fear of being suspected …

V. That others may be loved more than I,
R. *Jesus, grant me the grace to desire it.*
That others may be more esteemed than I …
That, in the opinion of the world, others may increase and I may decrease …
That others may be chosen and I set aside …

That others may be praised and I go unnoticed . . .
That others may be preferred to me in everything . . .
That others may become holier than I, provided that I may become as holy as I should . . .

Lord, grant me the grace of humility and charity, that I may love God above all things for Himself and be ready to renounce all created things rather than offend Him by serious sin. Amen.

Angelus

V. The angel of the Lord declared unto Mary
R. And she conceived of the Holy Spirit.
Hail Mary …

V. Behold the handmaid of the Lord;
R. Be it done unto me according to your word.
Hail Mary …

V. (Kneel) And the Word became Flesh
R. (Kneeling) And dwelt among us.
Hail Mary …

V. Pray for us O Holy Mother of God,
R. That we may be made worthy of the promises of Christ.

V. Let us pray:
R. Pour forth, we beseech You, O Lord, Your grace into our hearts, that we, to whom the Incarnation of Christ, Your Son, was made known by the message of an angel, may by His Passion and Cross be brought to the glory of His Resurrection, through the same Christ Our Lord. Amen.

Regina Caeli (to be prayed in place of the Angelus during the Easter Season)

V. Queen of Heaven, rejoice, alleluia.
R. For He Whom you did merit to bear,
alleluia.

V. Has risen, as He said, alleluia.
R. Pray for us to God, alleluia.

V. Rejoice and be glad, O Virgin Mary, alleluia.
R. For the Lord has truly risen, alleluia.

V. Let us pray:
R. O God, Who gave joy to the world through the Resurrection of Your Son, Our Lord Jesus Christ, grant, we beseech You, that through the intercession of the Virgin Mary, His Mother, we may obtain the joys of everlasting life. Through the same Christ Our Lord. Amen.

Divine Praises (to be prayed during Exposition and Benediction of the Most Blessed Sacrament or in thanksgiving at any time)

Blessed be God.
Blessed be His Holy Name.
Blessed be Jesus Christ, true God and true Man.
Blessed be the Name of Jesus.
Blessed be His Most Sacred Heart.
Blessed be His Most Precious Blood.
Blessed be Jesus in the Most Holy Sacrament of the Altar.
Blessed be the Holy Spirit, the Paraclete.
Blessed be the great Mother of God, Mary most holy.
Blessed be her holy and Immaculate Conception.
Blessed be her glorious Assumption.
Blessed be the name of Mary, Virgin and Mother.
Blessed be St. Joseph, her most chaste spouse.
Blessed be God in His angels and in His saints. Amen.

May the Heart of Jesus, in the Most Blessed Sacrament, be praised, adored, and loved with grateful affection, at every moment, in all the tabernacles of the world, even to the end of time. Amen.

Chaplet of Divine Mercy

Begin with the Sign of the Cross.

Pray once:

You expired, Jesus, but the source of life gushed forth for souls, and the ocean of mercy opened up for the whole world. O Fount of Life, unfathomable Divine Mercy, envelop the whole world and empty Yourself out upon us.

Repeat thrice:

O Blood and Water, which gushed forth from the Heart of Jesus as a fount of mercy for us, I trust in You!

Using a rosary, begin with one Our Father, one Hail Mary, and the Apostles' Creed.

On the Our Father beads pray:

Eternal Father, I offer You the Body, Blood, Soul, and Divinity of Your dearly beloved Son, Our Lord Jesus Christ, in atonement for our sins and those of the whole world.

On the Hail Mary beads pray:

For the sake of His Sorrowful Passion, have mercy on us and on the whole world.

Repeat thrice:

Holy God, Holy Mighty One, Holy Immortal One, have mercy on us and on the whole world.

Conclude with the Sign of the Cross.

Chaplet of St. Michael

Begin with the Sign of the Cross.

O God, come to my assistance. O Lord, make haste to help me. Glory be . . .

After each of the following salutations, pray one Our Father and three Hail Marys.

By the intercession of St. Michael and the celestial Choir of Seraphim, may the Lord make us worthy to burn with the fire of perfect charity. Our Father . . . Hail Mary . . .

By the intercession of St. Michael and the celestial Choir of Cherubim, may the Lord grant us the grace to leave the ways of sin and run in the paths of Christian perfection.

By the intercession of St. Michael and the celestial Choir of Thrones, may the Lord infuse into our hearts a true and sincere spirit of humility.

By the intercession of St. Michael and the celestial Choir of Dominions, may the Lord give us the grace to govern our senses and overcome any unruly passions.

By the intercession of St. Michael and the celestial Choir of Virtues, may the Lord preserve us from evil and falling into temptation.

By the intercession of St. Michael and the celestial Choir of Powers, may the Lord protect our souls against the snares and temptations of the devil.

By the intercession of St. Michael and the celestial Choir of Principalities, may God fill our souls with a true spirit of obedience.

By the intercession of St. Michael and the celestial Choir of Archangels, may the Lord give us perseverance in faith and in all good works in order that we may attain the glory of Heaven.

By the intercession of St. Michael and the celestial Choir of Angels, may the Lord grant us to be protected by them in this mortal life and conducted, in the life to come, to Heaven.

Pray one Our Father in honor of each of the following angels: St. Michael, St. Gabriel, St. Raphael, and your guardian angel.

O glorious prince St. Michael, chief and commander of the heavenly hosts, guardian of souls, vanquisher of rebel spirits, servant in the house of the Divine King and our admirable conductor, you who shine with excellence and superhuman virtue, deliver us from all evil, who turn to you with confidence, and enable us by your gracious protection to serve God more and more faithfully every day.

Pray for us, O glorious St. Michael, Prince of the Church of Jesus Christ, that we may be made worthy of His promises.

Almighty and Everlasting God, Who, by a prodigy of goodness and a merciful desire for the salvation of all men, has appointed the most glorious Archangel St. Michael Prince of Your Church, make us worthy, we ask You, to be delivered from all our enemies, that none of them may harass us at the hour of our death, but that we may be conducted by him into Your presence. We ask this through the merits of Jesus Christ Our Lord. Amen.

Litany of the Sacred Heart of Jesus

V. Lord, have mercy.
R. Lord, have mercy.
V. Christ, have mercy.
R. Christ, have mercy.
V. Lord, have mercy.
R. Lord, have mercy.
V. Christ, hear us.
R. Christ, hear us.
V. Christ, graciously hear us.
R. Christ, graciously hear us.

V. God, the Father of Heaven,
R. Have mercy on us.
God, the Son, Redeemer of the World ...
God, the Holy Spirit ...
Holy Trinity, one God ...

Heart of Jesus, Son of the Eternal Father ...
Heart of Jesus, formed by the Holy Spirit in the womb of the Virgin Mother ...
Heart of Jesus, substantially united to the Word of God ...
Heart of Jesus, of Infinite Majesty ...
Heart of Jesus, Sacred Temple of God ...
Heart of Jesus, Tabernacle of the Most High ...
Heart of Jesus, House of God and Gate of Heaven ...
Heart of Jesus, burning furnace of charity ...
Heart of Jesus, abode of justice and love ...
Heart of Jesus, full of goodness and love ...
Heart of Jesus, abyss of all virtues ...
Heart of Jesus, most worthy of all praise ...
Heart of Jesus, King and center of all hearts ...
Heart of Jesus, in Whom are all treasures of wisdom and knowledge ...
Heart of Jesus, in Whom dwells the fullness of divinity ...

Heart of Jesus, in Whom the Father was well pleased …
Heart of Jesus, of Whose fullness we have all received …
Heart of Jesus, desire of the everlasting hills …
Heart of Jesus, patient and most merciful …
Heart of Jesus, enriching all who invoke Thee …
Heart of Jesus, fountain of life and holiness …
Heart of Jesus, propitiation for our sins …
Heart of Jesus, loaded down with opprobrium …
Heart of Jesus, bruised for our offenses …
Heart of Jesus, obedient to death …
Heart of Jesus, pierced with a lance …
Heart of Jesus, source of all consolation …
Heart of Jesus, our life and resurrection …
Heart of Jesus, our peace and our reconciliation …
Heart of Jesus, victim for our sins …
Heart of Jesus, salvation of those who trust in You …
Heart of Jesus, hope of those who die in You …
Heart of Jesus, delight of all the saints …

V. Lamb of God, Who takes away the sins of the world,
R. Spare us, O Lord.
V. Lamb of God, Who takes away the sins of the world,
R. Graciously hear us, O Lord.
V. Lamb of God, Who takes away the sins of the world,
R. Have mercy on us, O Lord.
V. Jesus, meek and humble of heart,
R. Make our hearts like to Yours.

V. Let us pray:
R. Almighty and eternal God, look upon the Heart of Your Most Beloved Son and upon the praises and satisfaction which He offers You in the name of sinners; and to those who implore Your mercy, in Your great goodness, grant forgiveness in the Name of the same Jesus Christ, Your Son, Who lives and reigns with You forever and ever. Amen.

Litany of the Blessed Virgin Mary (Litany of Loreto)

V. Lord, have mercy.
R. Christ, have mercy.
V. Lord, have mercy on us. Christ, hear us.
R. Christ, graciously hear us.
V. God the Father of Heaven,
R. Have mercy on us.

V. God the Son, Redeemer of the world,
R. Have mercy on us.
V. God the Holy Spirit,
R. Have mercy on us.
V. Holy Trinity, One God,
R. Have mercy on us.

V. Holy Mary,
R. Pray for us.
Holy Mother of God …
Holy Virgin of virgins …
Mother of Christ …
Mother of the Church …
Mother of Mercy …
Mother of Divine Grace …
Mother of Hope …
Mother most pure …
Mother most chaste …
Mother inviolate …
Mother undefiled …
Mother most amiable …
Mother admirable …
Mother of good counsel …
Mother of our Creator …
Mother of our Savior …
Virgin most prudent …
Virgin most venerable …
Virgin most renowned …
Virgin most powerful …
Virgin most merciful …
Virgin most faithful …
Mirror justice …
Seat of wisdom …
Cause of our joy …
Spiritual vessel …
Vessel of honor …
Singular vessel of devotion …
Mystical Rose …
Tower of David …
Tower of ivory …
House of gold …
Ark of the Covenant …
Gate of Heaven …
Morning star …

Health of the sick …
Refuge of sinners …
Solace of migrants …
Comfort of the afflicted …
Help of Christians …
Queen of Angels …
Queen of Patriarchs …
Queen of Prophets …
Queen of Apostles …
Queen of Martyrs …
Queen of Confessors …
Queen of Virgins …
Queen of All Saints …
Queen conceived without Original Sin …
Queen assumed into Heaven …
Queen of the Most Holy Rosary …
Queen of families …
Queen of peace …

V. Lamb of God, Who takes away the sins of the world,
R. Spare us, O Lord.
V. Lamb of God, Who takes away the sins of the world,
R. Graciously hear us, O Lord.
V. Lamb of God, Who takes away the sins of the world,
R. Have mercy on us.
V. Pray for us, O Holy Mother of God,
R. That we may be made worthy of the promises of Christ.

V. Let us pray:
R. Grant, we beseech You, O Lord God, that we, your servants, may enjoy perpetual health of mind and body, and by the glorious intercession of the Blessed Mary, ever Virgin, may be delivered from present sorrow, and obtain eternal joy. Through Christ Our Lord. Amen.

Litany of St. Joseph

V. Lord, have mercy.

R. Christ, have mercy.

V. Lord, have mercy on us. Christ, hear us.

R. Christ, graciously hear us.

V. God the Father of Heaven,

R. Have mercy on us.

V. God the Son, Redeemer of the World,

R. Have mercy on us.

V. God the Holy Spirit,

R. Have mercy on us.

V. Holy Trinity, One God,

R. Have mercy on us.

V. Holy Mary,

R. Pray for us.

St. Joseph …

Renowned offspring of David …

Light of Patriarchs …

Spouse of the Mother of God …

Chaste guardian of the Virgin …

Foster father of the Son of God …

Diligent protector of Christ …

Head of the Holy Family …

Joseph most just …

Joseph most chaste …

Joseph most prudent …

Joseph most strong …

Joseph most obedient …

Joseph most faithful …
Mirror of patience …
Lover of poverty …
Model of artisans …
Glory of home life …
Guardian of virgins …
Pillar of families …
Solace of the wretched …
Hope of the sick …
Patron of the dying …
Terror of demons …
Protector of Holy Church …

V. Lamb of God, Who takes away the sins of the world,
R. Spare us, O Jesus.
V. Lamb of God, Who takes away the sins of the world,
R. Graciously hear us, O Jesus.
V. Lamb of God, Who takes away the sins of the world,
R. Have mercy on us, O Jesus.
V. He made him the lord of his household
R. And prince over all his possessions.

V. Let us pray:
R. O God, in Your ineffable Providence, You were pleased to choose Blessed Joseph to be the spouse of Your most holy Mother; grant, we beg You, that we may be worthy to have him for our intercessor in Heaven whom on earth we venerate as our protector: You who live and reign forever and ever. Amen.

Litany of the Tired Parent (by the Cowdens)

V. Lord, have mercy.
R. Christ, have mercy.
V. Lord, have mercy on us. Christ, hear us.
R. Christ, graciously hear us.

V. God the Father of Heaven,
R. Have mercy on us.
V. God the Son, Redeemer of the World,
R. Have mercy on us.
V. God the Holy Spirit,
R. Have mercy on us.
V. Holy Trinity, One God,
R. Have mercy on us.

V. Holy Mary,
R. Pray for us.
St. Joseph …
Holy angels …
Blessed saints …

V. From the evil of sin,
R. Deliver us, Jesus.
From the temptations around us …
From the glamour of the world …
From the distractions that abound …
From the deadly sin of pride …
From the deadly sin of greed …
From the deadly sin of lust …
From the deadly sin of envy …
From the deadly sin of gluttony …
From the deadly sin of wrath …
From the deadly sin of sloth …

V. For the will to seek You in all things,
R. Jesus, grant me the grace to desire it.

For the will to prefer Your ways over ours …
For the will to spend more time with You …
For the will to emulate the heroic virtue of the saints …
For the will to root out vice …
For the will to remain in union with You …
For the will to raise our children in the Faith …
For the will to orient our day around You …
For the will to make difficult decisions for our family …
For the will to be faithful …
For the will to be hopeful …
For the will to be charitable …
For the will to be patient …
For the will to be gentle …
For the will to be empathetic …
For the will to be merciful …
For the will to be generous …
For the will to choose virtue at all times …
For the will to be steadfast …
For the will to grow in love of You …

V. Lamb of God, Who takes away the sins of the world,
R. Spare us, O Lord.
V. Lamb of God, Who takes away the sins of the world,
R. Graciously hear us, O Lord.
V. Lamb of God, Who takes away the sins of the world,
R. Have mercy on us, O Lord.
V. Jesus, meek and humble of heart,
R. Make our hearts like to Thine.

V. Let us pray:
R: Lord, Who gave us the beautiful vocation of marriage and the gift of our children: Grant that we might always seek to do Your will, to follow the example of the saints, and to persevere in faith, that we might enjoy eternal Paradise with you forever in Heaven. Amen.

Prayer for a Mother

For mothers to pray:

Blessed Mother Mary, cover me with your mantle of love.
Help me to be patient.
Help me to be productive.
Help me to be joyful.
Help me to be present.
Help me to be prayerful.
Help me to be gentle.
Help me to be more like you,
Through your Son, Jesus Christ, Our Lord. Amen.

For fathers and children to pray:

Blessed Mother Mary, cover Mom with your mantle of love.
Help her to be patient.
Help her to be productive.
Help her to be joyful.
Help her to be present.
Help her to be prayerful.
Help her to be gentle.
Help her to be more like you,
Through your Son, Jesus Christ, Our Lord. Amen.

Passing Prayer

Blessed Mother Mary, cover Mom with your mantle of love.
Help her to be more like you. Amen.

Prayer of a Father

St. Joseph, you embody all the virtues I hope to attain through God's grace. I rely on your intercession and your guidance as I strive for holiness for myself and my family.

Adopt me as your spiritual son, so that I might learn from you.

Train me to hear God's voice and discern His will, you who heard God even while sleeping.

Take me to Egypt with you, along with my family, and protect us from the evil that wishes to harm us.

Help me to model purity and chastity for my family, that my children might be truly free to embrace God's vocation for them.

Show me how to exercise patience, that I might overcome my frustrations and embrace suffering.

Teach me holy silence, that my mind and my heart might be attuned to the presence of Jesus, especially in the Eucharist.

Lead me always to Jesus, that I might be able to gaze upon His Holy Face, in all its radiance, for all eternity.

I beg you, O glorious St. Joseph, to present my intentions before your Son, who always defers to you in holy obedience. Amen.

Passing Prayer

St. Joseph, adopt me as your spiritual son, so that I might learn from you. Amen.

Prayer for the Protection of the Angels

O powerful archangels, Sts. Michael, Gabriel, and Raphael, come to my assistance today.

St. Michael, help me to resist the empty promises of the devil and to fight for the glory of God's Kingdom.

St. Gabriel, help me to be attuned to God's voice and to live my vocation according to His will.

St. Raphael, help me to be open to the graces given to me in the sacraments, and cover me with the healing power of our mighty God.

Faithful archangels, do not leave my side. Amen.

Passing Prayer

Powerful archangels, do not leave my side. Amen.

Prayer for Married Couples

St. Gianna Molla, you modeled extraordinary love for your husband, your children, and God, and I'm leaning on you today to help me with my struggles. (*State your intention.*) I want to embrace the joys and sufferings of marriage and parenting, but I need help. Pray that I might grow to love my spouse and children more and more each day and that I will bear these burdens bravely and faithfully, as you did unto death. Amen.

Passing Prayer

St. Gianna Molla, pray that I will bear these burdens faithfully and bravely, as you did unto death. Amen.

Prayer of Couples Struggling with Infertility

God, we know that You are faithful. We know that You are loving. We know that You are all-powerful and all-good. We praise You for Your goodness. We praise You for Your compassion. We praise You for Your generosity. Through the intercession of Sts. Joachim and Anne, who saw Your generosity firsthand, we beg You to answer our prayers for (*Name*). May we, like Sts. Joachim and Anne, always be docile to Your plan and obedient to Your divine will, forever and ever. Amen.

Passing Prayer

Through the intercession of Sts. Joachim and Anne, Lord, we ask You to hear our prayers as we strive to conform to Your will. Amen.

Prayer for Grandparents

O God, we praise You and thank You for the gift of our grandparents, (*Names*). We are thankful for their wisdom, for their love, and for all the memories we've been able to make together. We ask you to watch over them this day, that they might be healthy, happy, and holy, and (*mention any other intentions*). We pray that, through the intercession of Sts. Joachim and Anne, they might enjoy the final years of their lives and, at the hour of their death, may be welcomed into Heaven to be with You forever. Amen.

Passing Prayer

God, thank You for the gift of our grandparents. Watch over them so they might be healthy, happy, and holy. Amen.

Prayer for the Conversion of Family Members

St. Monica, you persevered in prayer for your husband and your son, though it appeared to the world they were beyond the Lord's reach. I ask you to pray alongside me for the conversion of (*Name*). O faithful St. Monica, pray for my loved one as you prayed for St. Augustine. Amen.

Passing Prayer

O faithful St. Monica, pray for my loved one as you prayed for St. Augustine. Amen.

Prayer for an Impossible Cause

St. Rita, I come before you with a problem that feels impossible, a cause that seems lost. I don't know how this situation is going to turn out, and I'm struggling to (*find peace, keep the faith, remain patient, feel God's presence, etc.*). You are no stranger to suffering, and you were able to conform to the will of God, no matter what. Help me to bear this suffering, this thorn, with joy and love, so that I, too, may conform to God's loving will. Amen.

Passing Prayer

St. Rita, help me to bear this suffering, this thorn, with joy and love. Amen.

Prayer for the Healing of Family Rifts

St. Elizabeth, you know all too well the pain of family rifts. You worked for peace within your family. We ask you to come to our aid as we pray for (*state your need*). Help us to seek peace as you did, to speak with kindness, and to work toward reconciliation; and above all, help us to love God through loving one another more. Amen.

Passing Prayer

St. Elizabeth of Portugal, help us to heal our family rifts. Amen.

Prayer for a Lost Soul

O Holy St. Anthony, Hammer of Heretics, miracle-worker, and Doctor of the Church, you humbly lived your life in service of Christ, preaching truth in charity at a time when heresy persisted. St. Anthony, patron of lost souls, I ask you to keep in mind a particular lost soul (*Name*), who I fear is in danger of eternal punishment. O devotee of the Child Jesus, bring my prayer before Our Lord, that (*Name*) might be protected from harm and reconciled with our merciful Father. Amen.

Passing Prayer

St. Anthony, patron of lost souls, intercede for the conversion of (*Name*), who is in danger of eternal loss. Amen.

Prayer of a Parent during a Child's Tantrum

St. Thérèse, you know well the ups and downs of family life. You know that families are not perfect and that we sometimes resort to yelling and fighting. You also know that the family is the school of love, in which we learn charity, forgiveness, and self-control. Help me in the midst of this trial. Show me how to love God through my child. Help me to be patient, gentle, and compassionate. May this tantrum bring my child and me one step closer to Heaven. Amen.

Passing Prayer

St. Thérèse, show me how to love God through my child. Help me to be patient, gentle, and compassionate. Amen.

Prayer for the Person Who "Sanctifies" You

St. Josemaría Escrivá, you said it perfectly: "This person sanctifies me." Help me not to be bothered by this interaction, but help me to soften my heart so I can be sanctified. Remind me that everything I do should be oriented toward growing in holiness and getting to Heaven. Amen.

Passing Prayer

St. Josemaría Escrivá, help me to soften my heart so I can be sanctified by this interaction. Amen.

Prayer in Thanksgiving for Groceries

O God, through the example of St. Isidore the Farmer and Bl. Maria Torribia, You give us a beautiful example of a married couple's generosity and Christian charity. We thank You for the farmers who grew our food; for the truckers who transported it to the stores; for the grocers who stocked the shelves; and for the means by which we can afford this food. We thank You for our full fridge and full pantry. We ask that You bestow on us a greater sense of charity, that we, like Isidore and Maria, might be the best stewards of these gifts, always ready to share them with others. Amen.

Passing Prayer

O God, thank You for our full refrigerator and pantry. Inspire us to be more generous with what we have so that we may be ready to give and to help those who go without. Amen.

Prayer for Success in the Garden

St. Fiacre, skilled gardener and miraculous healer, thank you for your example of holiness as you used your vocation to serve the Lord. I ask that you watch over me as I work in my garden, not only for a successful yield but also that I might be ever aware of God's love for me. Like you, may I use my time to bring the love of God to my neighbor through my gardening. Amen.

Passing Prayer

St. Fiacre, skilled gardener and miraculous healer, watch over me as I work in my garden. Amen.

Prayer for Deceased Family Members

Eternal Father, I offer Thee the Most Precious Blood of Thy Divine Son, Jesus, in union with the Masses said throughout the world today, for all the holy souls in Purgatory, for sinners everywhere, for sinners in the universal Church, those in my own home and within my family. Amen.

Passing Prayer

Eternal rest grant unto (*Name*), O Lord, and let perpetual light shine upon him/her. May he/she rest in peace. Amen.

Prayer for the Grace to Forgive

Lord, I'm plagued by the hurt I've experienced in my life, and I'm finding it hard to want to forgive. I ask that, through the intercession of St. Josephine Bakhita, I might receive the graces necessary to forgive those who have hurt me. St. Josephine Bakhita, model of forgiveness, obtain for me the grace to forgive. Amen.

Passing Prayer

St. Josephine Bakhita, model of forgiveness, help me to pray for the grace to forgive. Amen.

Prayer for Your Parish Priest

Lord, I praise You for the gift of our priest, (*Name*). Watch over him and grant him the grace to be always faithful to You. May he love and serve our parish with a heart like St. John Vianney's, burning with love of You and love of his flock. Amen.

Passing Prayer

Lord, I praise You for the gift of our priest, (*Name*). Watch over him and grant him the grace to be always faithful to You. Amen.

Prayer of the Expectant Mother

St. Gerard, patron of unborn children and expectant mothers, I come to you with these concerns about my pregnancy (*state your concerns*). I ask that, through your intercession, I might find consolation and peace and place my trust and hope in the Lord. Pray for my unborn baby and me, for a safe and healthy delivery. Amen.

Passing Prayer

St. Gerard, patron of unborn children and expectant mothers, pray for my unborn baby and me. Amen.

Prayer for Chastity for the Entire Family

O Jesus, through the intercession of St. Thomas Aquinas, I pray for chastity and purity for my family. Guard our eyes, our minds, and our hearts from the stain of sin, and grant that we might surrender ourselves to Your will and Your will alone. Amen.

Passing Prayer

O Jesus, through the intercession of St. Thomas Aquinas, I pray for chastity and purity for my family. Amen.

Prayer for the Completion of Housework

St. Martin de Porres, the housework never really ends, does it? Help me find joy and satisfaction in the work I do to keep up my home. As I sweep the floors, help me to give thanks for the feet that walk along them. As I wash the dishes, help me to give thanks for the mouths that eat from them. As I dust the shelves, help me to give thanks for the faces in the photos that grace them. As I fold the clothes, help me to give thanks for the people who wear them. As I pick up the toys, help me to give thanks for my children, who play with them. Amen.

Passing Prayer

St. Martin de Porres, help me find joy in my housework. Amen.

Prayer for Perseverance amid Persecution

St. Teresa of Ávila, you bravely endured persecution out of love for truth. Help me in my trials today, as I, too, face ridicule for trying to live my Faith. Amen.

Passing Prayer

St. Teresa of Ávila, help me in my trials today. Amen.

Prayer While Assisting Someone Carrying a Cross

Jesus, You know well the pain of human suffering, because You experienced it in Your bitter Passion. Veronica, doing all she could, offered her veil to bring You comfort. Grant me the grace and the fortitude to extend that same selflessness to my neighbors as they carry their crosses. I offer my small acts of charity for love of You. Imprint your Face on my heart as I strive to ease the burdens of my neighbors. Amen.

Passing Prayer

Jesus, I offer my small acts of charity for love of You. Amen.

Prayer for a Family Enduring Mental Illness

Lord, be with us as our family endures the pain of (*mental illness, abuse, etc.*). This is a heavy cross, and we cannot bear it alone. Through the intercession of St. Dymphna, virgin and martyr, we pray for the grace to remain united as a family of faith, and we pray that this suffering will be for Your glory. Amen.

Passing Prayer

St. Dymphna, pray for us as we carry this cross together. Amen.

Prayer for an Ill Family Member

O Lord, through the intercession of St. Peregrine, we pray for healing for (*Name*), who suffers from (*state the illness*). In your mercy, hear our prayer. Heal us of our own physical and spiritual illnesses. We trust in Your goodness and pray for the grace to be ever more attuned to Your loving will. Amen.

Passing Prayer

O Lord, through the intercession of St. Peregrine, heal us of our physical and spiritual illnesses. Amen.

Prayer for Homemakers and Work-from-Home Parents

Sts. Louis and Zélie, I look to you for assistance with (*state your need*). Since you successfully raised five daughters who entered religious life, and since you modeled so beautifully the abandonment and trust required for Christian holiness, I ask with confidence for your heavenly friendship as I attempt to do the same in my life. Amen.

Passing Prayer

Sts. Louis and Zélie, I ask for your heavenly friendship today. Amen.

Prayer When Everything Is Going Up in Flames

St. Lawrence, you knew how to make the best of the worst situation. Please be with me as everything is going up in flames in my life. Help me approach this with a light heart, a sound mind, and a bit of humor. Remind me that the peace I seek can be found only when I surrender my will fully to Jesus Christ, our Savior. Amen.

Passing Prayer

St. Lawrence, be with me as everything is going up in flames. Amen.

Prayer in Thanksgiving for Coffee

Lord, I give You thanks for this cup of coffee. And though I feel I cannot do anything worthwhile without it, I know that I truly cannot do anything without You. Let this morning brew be a reminder to me that all I am and all I have is because of You. Please be patient with me today. I give my day to You, for Your glory. Amen.

Passing Prayer

Lord, I can't do anything without You. Use me for Your glory! Amen.

Prayer for Good Use of the Internet

Lord, You gave us Bl. Carlo Acutis to model Christian perfection in today's digital world. We ask that, through his intercession, we might be good stewards of our time and use the Internet in a way that pleases You. Amen.

Passing Prayer

Bl. Carlo Acutis, help us to use the Internet in a way that pleases God. Amen.

Prayer for Courage for Children

St. Kizito and St. José Sánchez del Río, you were both faithful to God, even when faced with death. Help me to be brave, even when it's hard. Help me to be faithful, even when I'm tempted. Help me to stay on the right path, even when others go down different paths. Be my friends and stay with me when I feel alone. Pray for me, so I can be happy in Heaven forever, like you. Amen.

Passing Prayer

St. Kizito and St. José Sánchez del Río, help me to be brave, even when it's hard. Amen.

Prayer for Our Friends

Lord, we thank You with great awe and sincerity for the gift of our friends. Through the intercession of St. John the Apostle, Your own beloved friend, we ask that You might shower our friends with an abundance of blessings and with the consolation of Your presence, now and forever. Amen.

Passing Prayer

Lord, thank You for the gift of our friends. Shower them with an abundance of Your blessings, now and forever. Amen.

Prayer for a Particular Need

O Holy St. Polycarp, disciple of St. John the Apostle, you were faithful to the gospel your entire life, even in the face of a brutal death. Since you know so well the glories and goodness of God, and since you have a reputation for literally putting out fires, I ask you to assist me in my need (*state your need*). Help me also to grow in friendship with the saints, as you did, so that together we may all enjoy eternal Paradise with Christ Our Lord. Amen.

Passing Prayer

St. Polycarp, help me to put out the fires that ravage my life. Amen.

Prayer to All Our Friends, the Saints

Lord, we praise You for the gift of the saints. Grant us the grace to be receptive to their teachings, to seek their constant company, to ask their intercession, and to desire the grace to join them in Heaven with You forever. All ye holy men and women, pray for us! Amen.